FOG:

An Analysis of Catholic Dogma

Garland Jaggers

Proctor Publications, LLC
Ann Arbor, Michigan

Proctor Publications, LLC
P.O. Box 2498
Ann Arbor, Michigan 48106
800-343-3034

Publisher's Cataloging in Publication
(Provided by Quality Books, Inc.)

Jaggers, Garland
        Fog : an analysis of Catholic dogma / Garland
Jaggers -- 1st ed.
        p. cm.
        Includes bibliographical references
        LCCN: 99-74302
        ISBN: 1-882792-79-3

        1. Catholic Church--Doctrines--Controversial
works. 2. Jaggers, Garland. 3. Afro-American
Catholics--United States--Biography. 4. Ex-Church
members--Catholic Church--Biography.   I. Title

BX1751.2.J34 1999   230.2
                    QBI99-736

Foreword

I was born rich. No! There was no silver spoon, family business, inheritance or land expanse to profit from. I was rich in another way.

I had parents with golden expectations, platinum ideas and pearlish wisdom.

This richness helped me survive, overcome, and triumph over the dogmatism (Fear, Blind Obedience, and Gloze - FOG) of Roman Catholic dogma.

In the end I profited richly from my parents. I gained a freedom of being, and of thinking that gave life its fullest and most profitable meaning. And now I can pass on to my children this same wealth.

I dedicate this book to:

The Gods in whose image I am created

Garland and Bennie Jaggers

and to the Gods created in my image

Howard, Leslie, Kim, and Melanie

ACKNOWLEDGMENTS

For a man, writing a book may be like a woman being pregnant and carrying her first child full term. Writing this book, at times, seemed to take control and precedence over my life. I became a prisoner to its completion and its completion was my release to freedom.

It, along with life and writing, is a long arduous journey, filled with the wonderment, doubt, and pain of creating. Yet, the expectation of that final delivery is so great that we struggle through the ugliness of our feelings – reality – and the labor of sleepless nights – drama. When it is all done and we have come to the time of delivery, and the product of our journey is here, we wipe away the tears, shrug off the fear and forget the doubt and pain. Now we remember only the fondness of the wonderful journey, and feel only the freedom of separation.

Here is the good that has happened to me. The good in the persons who helped me along this journey:

Walter T. Wallace, David Rambeau, Ron Milner, Ophelia Boyd, Betty DeRamus, Jamil Allah, Ivan Cotman and David Boone. The advice, criticism, guidance, and encouragement they gave me could be the subject of yet another book.

Upon reflection, I must thank, from my early days; Gladys for her courage in catechism class, Delores for her straightforwardness and candor, Mr. Dixon for his humor and genius ,and all my cronies for putting up with me.

Then, in my later years, there are the members of the board of the Office of Black Catholic Affairs who served without thanks and appreciation – without thanks or appreciation from the church – during my tenure as the Director;

William Porter, Archie Perry, Donald Robinson, Foster Wilson Jr., Jackie Currie, Deacon Allen McNeeley, Louis Smith, Regina Rambeau, Dorothy Howze, Manuel Howze, Jonas Johnson, Sharon Staff, Herman Sexton, Homer McClarty, Oreen Beard, Sandra Johnson, Betty L. Watson, Warrington Parker, Don Clark, Rufus Knighton, Maxine Knighton, Lee Bell, Claudette McMeekin, Pauline Adkins, Beverly Simmons, William Jenkins, David Rambeau, Leaviola Garris, Grace Jones, Gwen Kirksey, Brenda Smith, James Anderson, Agustine Comer, Cyril Nightingale, Fortaunates Lukanima, Philip Loving, Derby Fruge, William Mins, Thelma Williams, Fred Hunter, Clifford Thomas, Robert Lewis, Christella Perry, Louise Vaughn, Wallace D. Hill, Rita Hainsworth, Alma Hall, and Valerie Bennet.

INTRODUCTION

Martin Luther King, Jr. said in his classic work *Where Do We Go From Here?* (New York: Harper & Row, 1967, p.39);

"One of the greatest problems of history is that the concepts of love and power are usually contrasted as polar opposites. Love is identified with a resignation of power and power with a denial of love. What is needed is a realization that power without love is reckless and abusive and that love without power is sentimental and anemic."

This biography of my life in the Roman Catholic church is the story of my journey toward Martin Luther King, Jr.'s profound statement and understanding.

As a child I accepted the power of Roman Catholic dogma *sine quo non*. And that power, as exercised by the Priests, Bishops, et al, was abusive, reckless, and indifferent.

I found love in the fact that I was created in the image of the God of my father and my father's father, and caressed in the caring concerns of my mother, and my mother's mother.

While the concepts of love and power are clear, I now understand that the achievement of that *love power relationship* is what life is all about.

Chapter 1

Even to this day I can not forget that "fateful hour of truth."

I left the Renaissance restaurant high atop the hotel where Jertha and I had this long, intense two hour conversation about the crisis on my job as Director of the Office of Black Catholic Affairs.

I drove home, stopped at the local party store and picked up a six pack of E & B beer.

My house was pitch dark. I opened the front door and headed to the kitchen.

Janet, my wife, was in bed, as were my precious children, Leslie and Kim. I turned on the light, sat down at the kitchen table and popped the top of my first beer and took one l o n g thirst quenching swallow.

Ah h h h h h h – that was good.

When I set the bottle down, I thought: Jertha is one heavy brother.

I had just learned from Jertha – my friend, colleague, mentor, and religious savant – the arcane machinations of the Roman Catholic Church. These inside workings are seldom discussed and less often revealed to a select few in confidence. The truths that flowed from Jertha were shocking and unsettling; yet they articulated a reality that was painfully familiar. I knew, but did not want to know. Jertha had managed to relieve and discomfit me at the same time; his words had a ring of finality.

Finality, because I had no reason to disbelieve this well known, well read, world traveler and sage. With these revelations, I was forced to look back over my life in the church.

How had I gone astray? Who had misled me? And why had I let them? My mind raced from one event in my life to another. Little snatches of life rushed across my mind. I could not hold a thought for more than a second or two. Life was spinning around and around and upside down.

The clock on the kitchen wall read 11:55 pm.

As I drank my third beer, I pulled out some scraps of paper and a pencil and began to write. I wrote a poem. That was the easiest way to capture and express the emotional turmoil and mental anguish of the hour. Poetry expresses pain and confusion, doubt and resolution much clearer and easier than prose. And, prose would take too much time. I wrote:

> False Gods are dying.
>> Struck from their pedestal,
>> They leap frantically into the night
>> Seared by the blaze of truth.

False Gods are dying.
    Thrown against the pavement,
    Their fragile skin is ripped open
    And not an ounce of blood appears.
False Gods are dying.
    Melted by the heat of new days,
    Unechoing masses of smoldering metal
    Vanish in the steam.
False Gods are dying.
    Smelling of aged rot,
    Poisoned by another God
    Fouling mother nature's breath.
False Gods are dying.
    Killed by their own hands,
    Spun off into the universe
    Buried in infinity.
The last God is dying!

I wrote several poems, each expressing the pain, confusion, doubt and resolve of the hour, and each touching on one of the pivotal times when truth about the Roman Catholic Church was hidden and camouflaged, or when I turned a deaf ear and blind eye to fact and verity.

As each poem flowed through my pencil onto those scraps of paper, a new reality came into focus. It was now clear how I had gone wrong and who had led me there. It was now clear how I misread the truth.

I finished the last poem and the last beer and as my mind slowed almost to a snail's pace, I remembered.

3

I remembered all those special times in life which brought me back to my conversation with Jertha. I was struck with my life even as we spoke: a series of times of indoctrination, education, regimentation, and exploration.

And, now with his revelations, I have to go through a period of examination, confrontation, and change. Then, I have to move on.

The clock on the wall read 12:55 am. The hour of truth had ended.

My immediate recollection was of the very first day I started to attend Sacred Heart Catholic School.

Chapter 2

"Hey, Norm! What home room you gon' be in?"

"I don't know! Find out when we get there!"

"How you gon' get there, if you don't know where 'there' is?"

"It's in the school, fool." Delores chimed in. "He'll find it."

"Aw, girl, wasn't nobody talkin' to you."

I had mixed emotions as I started out to school that September morning in 1940. On the one hand, I wanted desperately to blend in with the bantering group of my neighborhood cronies. Take that right turn with them at the corner of St. Antoine Street and Livingston, and continue on to the familiar, raucous classrooms of Lincoln Elementary School. Go comfortably on to the familiar.

But, on the other hand, I had been entrusted with a mission; elevated to a new realm of responsibility. The dollar, first payment on my quarterly tuition, resting in my pocket, was a burning reminder of the weight I had now been committed to. My mother had made it very clear to me, my brother, and four sisters:

"We're paying this money for you all so you can get a better education. Be in a better environment. With more discipline. More order."

"You don't fool around with these Catholic people... these Nuns and Priests."

My father seconded that emotion.

"At 12 dollars a year, a piece, for each of you to go up there to that school – you'd ***best not*** be foolin' around. Wastin' my money."

So it was with a more serious focus and commitment than in my previous year at Lincoln School that I, at seven, headed for the second grade, turned *left* at the corner, and waved good-bye to, and walked away from, the familiarity of Lincoln – and headed for the unknown at Sacred Heart Catholic School.

I could see on the faces of my siblings that they too were feeling the weight of this new direction, costing our parents so much sacrifice. Even Rhodie Ellen and Maxine, running up ahead in their eternal game of skip and tag, would now and again settle into a thoughtful steady pace, their brown lunch bags swinging by their sides. Rhodie Ellen and Maxine, like me, fell silent as soon as we turned the corner away from Lincoln.

I shared their apprehension, but remembering the stern but hopeful expression on our parents' faces, I mentally squared my shoulders and firmed my determination to succeed in this new thing looming up ahead.

Sacred Heart: As soon as you pushed open the tall wooden oak doors and went up the stairs, you were immediately struck by the first significant difference between here and my previous school: the silence. Silence was the rule rather than, as at Lincoln, the exception. Relative silence even in the hallways; where Mama's desired discipline and structure was actually tangible, visible, controlled, and punctuated every thirty yards or so by those white-peaked, black robed figures of correctness – the Nuns, the Sisters.

"Young man, here at Sacred Heart we do not slam doors. We op-pen and clo-se them, qui-et-ly."

(Sisters was the perfect descriptive term for them, for like your blood sisters, the fact that they were females was not to be too deeply contemplated. And, like your true sisters, they could also do you in with a bad report to "Father.")

Yes, Father. That was how the Priest was introduced to us: Father. Father Klein. And he was a revelation in power and symbolism. For all their apparent correctness, the Sisters bowed completely to the will and word of Father. They explained to us why this was. Father was our local embodiment of an upward spiraling line of Fathers going from here at Sacred Heart on the Eastside of Detroit, on up around and through the city, the country, the world; through a succession of Fathers, Priests, Cardinals and Bishops, all the way up to THE Father on earth, the Pope in Rome. The Pope being a direct intermediary of THE Father of all things, Our Father Who Art In Heaven: God Himself. And as our Father in Rome, the Pope, represented and interpreted the will of Our Father in heaven, our Father there at Sacred Heart represented and interpreted for us the will of our Father there in Rome. In short, there was a "divine line" leading from God through the Pope to the Father at Sacred Heart. A divine line comprised of white, male, Catholic representatives of the Divine Father. The suggestion being that God was male, white, and – – Catholic. Reacting to such a psychological impact, what could an eager and ambitious, seven year old little Black boy do to be in the good graces, and heed the words, of such power figures?

To please Father one had to know and observe the Catechism. In 1905, after a call from the Pope for renewed efforts in recruitment and indoctrination, many United States parishes began to teach what was called the Baltimore Cathechism: 499 edicts of the church. With such pronouncements as, "if you missed one Sunday mass and did not confess this 'sin' to Father, you were assigned to hell forever!" Forever! For missing once! When we students asked Father why there were 499 pronouncements and not five-hundred, he answered that the five-hundredth was "The Mystery..."

Ah, yes, one of the many mysteries of the church.

Chapter 3

The Catechism and the confessional. I cannot count the times from 1943 until I graduated in 1950 that I stood in the confessional line behind the other students at Sacred Heart Church, located just east of Hastings Street (the boulevard of Detroit's Black community) at Eliot Street, and rehearsed the words, "Bless me Father, for I have sinned . ." Waited my turn to go into the dark cubicle to confess to Father who hid in his cubicle behind a small shuttered door and a semi-sheer black curtain. *Dark, shuttered cubicles: Again the deep dark mysteries. Very impressive to a still forming young mind.* First I recited my mortal sins; those considered "a grievous sin against the law of God," which condemned you to Hell should you die without confession – like missing a Sunday Mass. Next, I would recite the venial sins; those considered less offensive. Those that would send you to purgatory if you die without confession – like telling a lie. I would end with, "I am sorry for these and all the sins of my past life." Father would require that I do penance to prove my sincerity and gain atonement. "Recite the rosary four times. Go in peace; your sins are forgiven."

To comprehend the power and importance of the Baltimore Catechism you have to know that we were neither taught from the Bible in school, nor allowed to read it for ourselves. The explanation given was that only Father could correctly interpret the Bible. So my child's mind assumed that the Bible must have been written in some strange, difficult, foreign, hard to decipher language. Later, in college, I would learn that the Council of Trent, circa 1545, had strongly 'discouraged' Bible reading for the average Catholic.

Faithfully, Father would appear every Tuesday for our class in Catechism. During these classes we could raise any question we wanted with regard to our Catholic teachings. For me these sessions might have been entitled, "Hearing the Father Answer All The Questions I Didn't Dare To Ask." The one who dared most was Gladys, a very pretty, taller and more-developed-than-average twelve year old. (Upper and lower grades sometimes shared certain classes and classrooms). Looking back on it, I think Gladys was also more developed mentally, and as to intestinal fortitude, was ahead of us all. She would lock eyes with Father seated at Sister's desk, and challenge him with her questions.

"Now, Father, you say that only those baptized Catholic and free of mortal sin can get in heaven. Right? . . . Uh huh. So what about all those people who were born before Christ came?" Others would chime in:

"Yeah. What about little children who die at birth, like, before they can get baptized?"

"All the people all around the world who haven't been exposed to Catholicism? All the people of other faiths? Are they all condemned to hell?" Gladys would ask.

"None of them can get into heaven. Only Catholics." Father would answer. When he was really strapped for an answer to a particularly tough question, Father would retreat to his safe reply, "These are part of the mysteries of our faith." Sometimes you could hear the girls chanting this old tired answer under their breath, ". . . the mysteries of our faith . . Yeah . ."

The boys would approach more from the theological front, thereby revealing that someone had been reading the bible somewhere: "You mean everyone, absolutely everyone, on the face of the earth except Noah and his family were sinful and needed to be drowned?"

"Yeah, and like if Noah and his family were the only ones left, like, they were like, the mothers and fathers of us all just, like Adam and Eve, right ?"

"Uh huh. So Noah and his folks were baptized Catholics by who? Whoever it was must've died, right? Since Noah and them were the only good people left, right?"

"Naw, they were like Moses, they came before Christ so they can't get in heaven anyway. Right, Father? . ."

"Well, why were they saved then . . . ?"

Father would give his standard answers and stalls, until the bell rang saving his composure for another week.

Once – I suppose he wanted us to believe and understand his power – Father told the story of Emperor Henry IV, who stood in the snow at Canossa begging for forgiveness from Pope Gregory VII who threatened to excommunicate him for thwarting his edict. The story brought silence to the class – but just for a moment.

Mom listened intently to what we were learning. Dad was usually still at his second job. In retrospect I can now remember how her face became an impassive mask when we mentioned that we weren't taught, and weren't allowed to read, the Bible. Years later she would tell us how she had held her peace for the sake of a better "basic education." I seem to recall my dad once saying something to the same effect, "If they want to learn about the Bible, they can ask me. My mother had me in that Pentecostal church learnin' it all day long sometimes."

They were paying twelve-dollars a child, for six of us, seventy-two dollars a year, (rent on our four bedroom flat was only $10 per month) for us to go to Sacred Heart; it wasn't for the catechism: It was to get us better prepared for this world here on earth.

I let the others question the catechism, my job was clear: I had to excel at learning everything, including the catechism. That was what my parents were paying for. I had to learn and achieve. The path to succeeding was obviously through the catechism; and although I had no Baptist upbringing, I knew early how to "keep my eye on the prize." I did not know then that what you accept into your head gets into your system and can sometimes create "cancers." Some of the church dogma I accepted became akin to spiritual cancers.

I think I was always a focused overachiever. I acquired a paper route with the *Detroit Times* when I was eleven years old and worked it up from a 72 to a 250 customer route – much like having one thousand customers today. In seven years I earned 7 trips to other cities by virtue of my efforts in new customer recruitment. I traveled to more big cities than either of my parents. I saw Old Ironsides in Boston, stood atop the Empire State Building in New York, strolled the Broadwalk in Atlantic City, touched the Liberty Bell in Philadelphia, rode a steamship to Niagra Falls, traveled by train to Cleveland, and shopped at Marshall Fields in Chicago.

I am sure my successes and my positive approach to life and my capabilities came from both my parents and my nurturing home environment.

I was raised by a hard-working, inventive, self-educated, World War I veteran father, Garland Jaggers, Sr. and a beautiful, disciplined, God-loving caring mother, Bennie (named after her father Benjamin). As I stated before, I grew up around Hastings Street. Hastings' reputation carried with it an undercurrent of nefariousness. Well, perhaps that was its nighttime character, but for a kid it was an open-air market of goodies, a bazaar, a "moving feast" of a life symposium. Movie theatres – The Warfield Castle and Willis come quickly to mind for our area of the boulevard – vegetable stands, fish markets, chicken markets, restaurants, clothing stores; a virtual riot-chorus of curb side philosophers providing a running commentary on the do's and don'ts of life. Our block was full of friendly, fun filled, caring people – adult and youngsters. I can only remember two fights over all those years. One year, our block won the Clean Block Campaign, sponsored by the *Michigan Chronicle*, a Black owned local weekly newspaper – which was quite an accomplishment considering that our next door neighbor raised chickens in his back yard.

My dad's best friend was a mechanic named Mr. Dixon, who to this day I consider a genius. Although, he only had a tenth-grade education, somehow he knew the principles of algebra, geometry, and calculus. He could fix any car, truck, or horse cart ever made. There was always a line of people with their vehicles waiting for Mr. Dixon outside his shop. But at dark, regardless of the line of business outside his shop, he would stop working on cars and trucks to work on his pet project: A PERPETUAL MOTION MACHINE! I can still see his contraption whirling around in the basement of his house: A wheel spinning and climbing up this elaborately balanced ramp of cogs. Having reached the top of his ramp, it would begin its decline along a down ramp. I was sure that one day he would complete his contraption and become very rich and famous.

Mr. Dixon got a kick out of both my admiration for his genius and my irritation at being called Junebug (nickname for Junior). As I hung around his shop watching him work his magic – once he diagnosed the trouble with an engine by listening to it through a stick – he couldn't resist calling me Junebug. Constantly. In my first win-win negotiation I told him one day that every time he called me Junebug he would have to pay me a penny. He agreed!

"Okay, Junebug: Here's your penny," he laughed.

He continued to call me Junebug and pay for the privilege. Which was a good deal for me. A penny bought a pocket full of candy in the mid-forties.

Chapter 4

Meanwhile I was working hard on the "deal" of becoming a Catholic. At the time of my Confirmation (a rite of passage signifying conscious commitment), Father came to catechism class to approve the name each confirmee had selected for confirmation. It was the custom for students to select the name of the saint whose qualities he/she liked, and whose virtues he/she wanted to emulate. I admired the virtues of Blessed Martin De Porres and wanted to emulate him, so I chose the name Martin.

Well, Father disallowed this name because Martin De Porres was only "Blessed." He was not yet a Saint. Blessed Martin De Porres was the only black face I found among the slim list of Saints provided by Father. So I made a trip to the Main Library to see if I could find a Black saint. In the year 1945 I could not find any Black person elevated to sainthood by the Catholic Church. That raised a jagged question in the back of my mind about the Church and myself as a Black person. But it was a question I couldn't afford to pursue and still concentrate on my mission of being successful as a Catholic. Also, I did not have the kind of sophistication and knowledge I would need in order to answer such a question. I was going purely on gut reaction. And what my gut told me at that time was that I needed to deal with this the way I had dealt with Mr. Dixon's Junebug. I selected the name Martin for confirmation, and told father it was for a St. Martin of France, a white Saint I had discovered at the library. I lied. I can now confess that it was Martin De Porres, not St. Martin of France, whom I'd chosen.

I now regret my subterfuge. I should have confronted the issue like Gladys. Yet, had he understood my need for a Black role model, Father had several options. One option would have been to tell me about the THREE BLACK POPES (St. Victor I, St. Melchiades, and, St. Gelasius) who presided over the church. (Had Father forgotten this fact? Or had he never known it? Why, with his German background, did Father Klein not tell me of the Black Saint Maurice of Germany, one of the most highly regarded Saints of the Holy Roman Empire?) Another option would have been to provide us with a more complete list of saints as there were many who were Black. Neither me nor my classmates could bring this explosive issue to the catechism class, for we lacked the knowledge.

Notwithstanding my subterfuge, I scored high on all the tests in catechism class and was given the privilege of being an altar boy.

Altar boys assist the Priest by doing a number of tasks before, during, and after mass. They respond in Latin (memorized by rote) to the various incantations chanted by the priest, prepare the altar before mass, light the candles, fill the decanters with wine and water, hold the paten under the chin of those receiving Holy communion, lock the doors after mass, and put away the vestments worn by the priest during mass.

To be honest, I loved serving as an altar boy. Especially serving at High Mass, when we would light the fragrant incense, engulfing the entire altar in the sweet aroma of burning perfume.

I often served along with another all "A" catechism student named Sylvan Vasconcellos (a go getter like myself who lived in the hard-to-get-in Brewster projects near school). Father preferred two altar boys at each mass, sometimes four if it were a High Mass. Sylvan and I would compete with each other for accuracy and artistry of response to father's incantations.

"Dominos Vobiscum," Father would chant.

"Et cum spiritu tuo," Sylvan and I would respond in melodic unison.

When Father "raised the host", one of us had to ring the chimes. There was an art to the ringing of the chimes. I liked to ring them softly, at first; increase the sound as Father raised the host; decrease the sound as he lowered it. Similarly, I used the same technique when he raised and lowered the chalice. (This point in the mass was for me the most dramatic part of the ceremony, the moment Christ came down from heaven and became the host and wine – symbolically the body and blood of Christ.)

Each day of the week there were two morning masses, at 7:30 and 8:30. During the 7:30 mass there were usually only two or three people in church, sometime none. It made no difference to Father, Sylvan or me, even when the church was empty. We took our duties and performances seriously. Besides, Father had his back to the people in the pews during most of the mass. He was in his own world, little concerned about the people in the pews or Sylvan and I.

Two things did unsettle me a bit, though. One, while I knew the correct Latin response, I did not know what I was saying. I just learned the response by rote memory. It seemed rather silly to be speaking a language I did not understand and to be saying I didn't know what. Two, while serving mass Father seemed sometimes rather tipsy – especially when he had to drink all the wine left in the chalice.

But one thing about being an altar boy made both me and Sylvan happy; when we served the 8:30 mass we could be late for school! We never broke any speed records tidying up things and reporting to class afterwards.

Under the Baltimore Catechism all masses were said in Latin, and the Priest always had his back to the people. Thus, the mass itself was rather routine and lifeless; the church would be deathly quiet even when filled with people. But Sylvan and I honestly believed we added livening highlights with our perfectly tuned and timed responses, and our robot-like movements around the altar.

Once while illuminating the Baltimore Cathechism Father told us, "If you are in an emergency situation where a person is seriously hurt, and you believe the person might die, and there is no Priest around for miles and miles, and you feel the person might die before a Priest can arrive, anyone may and should baptize that person." I don't know how the other catechists felt, but for me it was empowerment. I could have the same power as Father – the power to baptize. (And in my thirtieth year I did in fact baptize an individual.)

Father cautioned us however that such an emergency baptism was only temporary. Should the person survive the accident he/

she should go to a Priest for a *real* baptism (?). He did not say how long the emergency baptism would last, when it would "wear off" as it were.

There was one catechistic declaration in particular, and Father's so called "clarification" of it, that constantly got me in hot water with my Protestant friends back home, and later with my own mind. The telling part of the "credo" read: . . . Jesus Christ . . who suffered under Pontius Pilate, was crucified, died, and was buried. He descended into *hell*. The questions I was afraid (perhaps petrified) to ask in catechism were: "Why do we say Christ descended into hell? Why did He go there? What did He do there? With whom did He speak? Who wrote this 'Apostles' Creed'? What is this all about?"

Father had his stock answers from the Baltimore Catechism: "When we say that Christ descended into hell, we mean that, umm, after he died, the soul of Christ descended into the place, umm, a state of rest, called limbo, where the souls of the just were, umm, waiting for him." (Father's simple answer may have worked in Catechism class but it will not work now, given my new knowledge. The "Apostles' Creed" was not written by the apostles, therefore it is misnamed and misleading. Since the creed was written by early Christians making a statement of faith, what did they really mean then? If the truth is that he did not go to hell, why don't we just change the Apostles' Creed so that it speaks what it means? Let us just say that he descended into limbo and be done with it.)

My non-Catholic, teenaged friends often just laughed at me when I attempted to explain limbo.

"Garland, fool, when you die you either go to heaven or hell.

That's it. Limbo's somethin' you Catholics made up just to be different." Delores would say.

While we all agreed on the existence of Heaven and Hell, the idea of limbo and purgatory were unknown, laughable concepts to my non-Catholic friends. Father would have us understand that limbo was a place of suspended animation. Babies who died without baptism, people who died before Christ's resurrection (Adam, Eve, Abel, Noah, Moses, Soloman and each and every soul mentioned in the Bible who had lived a decent life, included) had to sit in limbo because the doors of heaven were closed.

"The doors of heaven were closed?" Delores asked laughing.

"The doors of heaven were closed?" Norman and Joyce joined in.

Delores could not contain her laughter. So, she went home bent over in laughing tears. Norm and Joyce followed.

No wonder my friends laughed. Limbo was too much of a stretch, and the doors being closed was just too funny.

Strangely enough, Father seldom talked about Heaven, that goal we all wanted to achieve. But back on Illinois Street I heard Delores, Norman and Joyce talk about St. Peter and the pearly gates and the land of milk and honey. Father did talk about purgatory, where most people not destined for Hell had to stop over and atone for all their venial sins. It was a place of punishment one should avoid if possible.

I have to admit that in those early, naive and innocent years the concept of purgatory was more palatable to me than that of limbo. Purgatory was reserved for all those baptized who died with a venial sin on their souls. (Venial sins were not so egregious that they would condemn one to hell)! The church in its wisdom and mercy had set up an elaborate indulgence system of earning credit for time to be spent in purgatory when you die. It was much like the "good time off" system that prisoners earn while in jail. But in this case one earned the time here on earth: So many days or weeks or 'years' of "good time off" in purgatory for certain good acts or prayers. For example, making the sign of the cross, saying, "In the name of the Father, and of the Son, and of the Holy Ghost, Amen" earned you 100 days of indulgence (time off) in purgatory. If you made the sign of the cross with Holy Water, you got three-hundred days indulgence. There were literally hundreds of things you could do to gain indulgence; ranging from a few days to years. Reciting the prayer, "Hail, Holy Queen," earned 5 years.

Feeling sorrow and pity for all of the many souls sitting in purgatory suffering, my young mind developed a scheme to get some of them out. I would do all these things accumulating "good time" and credit them to whoever had been in purgatory longest. I figured in my at once, political, yet naive, mind that if I helped someone get out they would in good turn intercede for me.

In my later studies I learned, to my horror and disgust, that the indulgence system became so corrupt during the early church years that Priests often gave indulgence in exchange for money. Much of the Church's early wealth is traceable to this cash-and-carry system of indulgence granting.

Long before turning up this knowledge, the indulgence system appeared fatally flawed to my common sense reasoning on some very simple points: 1) The system guaranteed that if you received Holy Communion on nine consecutive first Fridays of the month you were guaranteed a priest at your bedside at death, making

God an accountant who kept time according to man's watch and calendar (presumptuous at best); 2) The indulgence system almost guaranteed heaven (I cannot believe heaven can be so easily accessed by some number of prayer recitations or deeds).

Chapter 5

Delores, who was my first girl friend, and who lived right across the street from me, became incensed with me when in following rule #205 of the Baltimore Catechism, "A Catholic sins against faith by taking part in non-Catholic worship because he thus professes a belief in a religion he knows is false," I declined to attend her church services with her. She set fire to me: "You can't even go to your own Catholic Church over there on Leland Street. The white folk at St. Wienueski just two block from here won't let you in." Delores always goes straight to the point (or the jugular) in an argument, "Since you can't go to another Catholic church, why are you banned from a Protestant church? Are you banned from all churches except Sacred Heart church?"

I hid my discomfort behind a mysterious, superior smile I had picked up from some actor (maybe David Niven at the Castle theater). She was right. St. Wienueski was a Polish church sitting smack dab in the middle of our black neighborhood, a half-block from where we lived, and we could not attend mass there. After giving her the plastic smile, I told her that Catholic Black folks had to put up with the same things other Black folks did – but

God was on our side. She quietly walked away, having delivered a telling blow, and left me alone for a few days.

Chapter 6

It is utterly amazing to me that neither Mom or Dad ever confronted our teaching in Catechism class, irrespective of the differences they had with that indoctrination. Especially in view of the conversations we had later on. Dutifully, silently, they attended all the plays, special masses, baptisms, confirmations, and weddings of their children at school and church. Attended proudly, with dignity, and in full support of their children. I suspect they had decided to wait and see how each of their six children would interpret and handle the teachings in their respective adult lives.

I graduated from Sacred Heart High School with top honors in my class and applied for admission to Wayne State University. And the ease and security of my youth was in one moment shattered to pieces! On September 1st, 1950 the admissions officer at Wayne informed me that Sacred Heart High School was not accredited and that to be admitted to Wayne State as a full time student I would have had to take the entrance exam for which I was late. Being at the top of my class at Sacred Heart meant absolutely nothing at Wayne State.

I remember walking in a stunned and blinding rage. Walking

east, back in the direction from which I had come; down Hancock Street where I now lived, then turning south and again east, heading back to the beginning, toward Illinois Street and Sacred Heart and all those foolish wasted years. I could hear Delores and all the others from the neighborhood who had considered me a snobbish Catholic fool, laughing at me royally now! What had Father and the Sisters at Sacred Heart been preparing me for? What about all that money my parents had scraped up for this "better" education? Father and Sister had to know – had to! Why hadn't they told us, warned us? I walked on seeing or hearing nothing but my own thoughts. But gradually I turned to the old, old rationale: It wasn't Father's fault, Catholic's fault – it was the society, the racist society. If I had received top honors from Catholic Central with its Irish, Polish, and French extraction students, I would be accredited. But coming from Sacred Heart, an all-Black Catholic student body, my honors meant nothing. Yes, it wasn't Father's fault. It was this racist society! Well, I would show them that grades from Black Sacred Heart were just as valid as from Catholic Central, Cass Tech, or any other school! I marched back to Wayne State's admissions office and signed up as a non-matriculated student!

I took six credit classes; then eventually took the entrance exam, passed it, and became a full-time student. Eureka! A whole new world opened up for me!

It is easy for me to say that I experienced culture shock: From an all Black school, I stepped into a partially integrated, but mostly white student body. For the first time in my educational experience I was in a classroom with more than 15 students. In fact, our science class held about 120 students – more than the total number of students at Sacred Heart High! And in some classes I was the only Black enrolled. White students I found were not very friendly when it came to competition. Competition was tough! It was dog-eat-dog except for those who belonged to in-groups like fraternities and sororities and other campus clubs, enjoying a special status among the student body. For the first time in my academic life I had to really study hard. Some students skipped classes and still got the "A" grade, others seemed to have pre-knowledge of tests, and many professors seemed to have class favorites. I fit none of these categories. I simply had to hit the books hard, rest, get up and hit them again.

I came to understand the adages that there is power in groups, psychological safety in numbers, osmotic knowledge in networks – and joined a fraternity. Kappa Alpha Psi. Soon my argumentative, authoritative personality made me the coach of the championship intramural basketball team. My ability to research thoroughly made me a good debater, and source of homework answers. In short, I began to have a place, a persona, on campus.

Unlike what Father had told us, that life revolved around heaven and hell, at Wayne I came to understand that religion and all other pursuits and endeavors resolved around life, relationships, people, family, happiness, work, maturation, graduation.

The intellectual give and take was dizzying for one whose education had been dominated by the Catholic dogma of Catechism class, with all questioning stifled with Father's catchall answer, "That is part of the mystery of our faith." And why were they mysteries, we would ask?

"Mysteries are things beyond our understanding which we must believe because of our faith."

In the questioning, exchanging, discovering atmosphere of

Wayne's campus, the frats, and surrounding environs, my mind and my sense of selfhood began to expand and lift like some giant helium filled balloon.

One day I came face to face with this startling combination of beauty, charm, intelligence and sensuality named Janet Swayne. Before long I was collecting and spouting poetry; reveling at every flash of approval in those grey-green eyes. I felt my heart skip a beat or two, and knew early on that she would be my wife. But there were a few sticky moments. Janet's family were Jehovah Witnesses and the first time I kept her out past curfew and brought her to her front door, all set to disarm her mother (who waited up for her) with my poetic charm and intellect, Mrs. Swayne startled me by taking a swing at me! Thank God I ducked, she missed. I beat a hasty retreat and decided to do my peacemaking from a distance, over the phone, concentrating on her father, Mr. Swayne. (Who was to remain my ally over the coming years).

Mr. Swayne (I lovingly called him Pa Swayne) fascinated me. He could quote from the Bible (the taboo book of my youth) and make cross references in it like quicksilver. I had never before met a person so intensely involved in religion (except Father who never quoted the Bible). It was not unusual for Pa Swayne to corner me, while Janet primped, powdered, and bejeweled herself for our date, and give me a lesson or two from the Bible. I listened intently, first because he was to be my future father-in-law, and then because his understanding of the Bible was differently focused. Pa Swayne knew I was Catholic; he did not hold it against me, yet he did share his view of the Catholic Church with me, "They are imposters, those Catholics. IMPOSTERS!"

It was while I was in college that I dared to attend a non-

Catholic church. I was shocked! Much of what they said and talked about was the same as we did in Catholic church – and their service was in English! What a relief that was; making the service both more interesting and understandable. The music played in the Protestant Church made the services also more lively, not likely to lull you to sleep as some Catholics were often seen to do in our church. But the most startling thing was the fact that nearly everyone had a <u>Bible</u>! Were able to examine the Word for themselves. Were able to question, agree or disagree with the "Father" of their church. Amazing!

This new found freedom to ask questions and expect reasoned answers allowed me to also attend Jewish, Seventh Day Adventist, Ba Hai, and Mormon services. . . and so on. As a matter of fact I never turn down an invitation to attend the churches of other faiths. (Delores would be proud of me) I take such invitations to mean they want me to come and meet their GOD. So out of respect for the invitee and out of personal inquisitiveness I go, frequently to great surprise, pleasure, and instruction.

One of the more memorable subjects discussed in catechism class is the adage, "Turn the other cheek." The truth of the matter is that this adage is found in Matthew 5:8 thru 42. Matthew says: "Ye have heard that it has been said, an eye for an eye and a tooth for a tooth: *but I say* unto you that ye resist not evil: but whosoever shall smite thee on thy right cheek turn to him the other also: And if any man shall sue thee at law, and take away thy coat, let him have thy cloak also. And whosever shall compel thee to go a mile go with him twain. Give to him that asketh thee and to him that asketh thee turn thou not away."

It is clear to me now that neither Father nor the Church have followed this admonition by Matthew. And this reality leads to other questions.

How many of us remember the school bully who continued to harass, steal from, and intimidate little kids until someone stood up to him? How does Matthew suggest we handle the bully? Turn the other cheek? And what about your neighbor who borrows your lawn mower but never returns it? Do you go and buy another? Or sue? Turn the other cheek? Is this what Matthew intended? I wonder.

I testify that I now believe that injustice is evil and must be confronted. I testify that I believe, "turn about is fair play." I testify that self-defense is nature's law. I testify that kids on my block, and even some in our Catechism class, would say, "Do unto others before they do you!" (I confess, I have not yet reached that point in my own understanding and belief.)

If we accept Father's interpretation of, "do unto others as you would have others do unto you, turn the other cheek, etc." we become passive players in life, subject to, and at the whim and will of those who choose to steal from us, disrespect us, or trample over our lifespace. Each of us, I now believe, is responsible for peace and justice in our lifespace, and by expansion, in the world. Father would have no such argument in Catechism class: We must be forgiving, humble, non-aggressive, silent and meek. But, he demonstrated none of these virtues! (*Do as I say, not as I do!*)

What would Matthew, or for that matter, Father, have had me do when as Director of Black Catholic Affairs, I witnessed the cover up of one of the most despicable acts known to mankind, pedophilia, take place in the society of the Catholic Church?

A suburban Priest was accused of pedophilia and jailed. This story appeared on the front pages of the local newspapers. I waited to see how the Church would react to this allegation. The silence in the Church bureaucracy was deafening. Not one lay person or Priest in the main offices on Michigan Avenue said a word. I waited and listened; listened and waited. The conspiracy of silence was complete.

Finally I read in the paper that the Priest had been sent to Europe for psychiatric rehabilitation. The article, <u>on the back page</u>, was brief with no details of the court proceedings. Perhaps the legal staff of the Church had cut a deal. The thought of the child and his family being counseled to "turn the other cheek" filled me with outrage at the possibility. This Priest's alleged actions and the handling of the matter by the Church flew in the face of justice, openness and atonement. Perhaps the child assaulted by the Priest was given therapy/treatment and the parents paid off, as has been done in so many cases. Is this cover up "turning the other cheek?" I think not.

It pains me to know that somewhere in the world some pedophile Priest (and their numbers have been documented) may be molesting another child, and the Church again paying off the family with the nickels and dimes donated to the Church by the poor believing laity. But nowhere in the world (though lately, most grudgingly) do I hear the Church owning up to its crimes against children. Does the church now insist that the victim "turn the other cheek?"

But all this takes me years ahead of the previous moment in my story.

Chapter 7

During my last year of college (1956) I secured full-time employment with the City of Detroit Welfare Department, taking night classes to complete the required number of hours for graduation.

I never envisaged or dreamed of serving in the army. As a college student I applied for and got the "college student deferment" from the draft. Deep down in my heart I felt that once called for the draft, (after I received my degree), I had an ace up my sleeve. I had flat feet and would not pass the physical. Imagine my surprise when the army physician, noting my flat feet, checked the appropriate box, and stamped my physical PASSED! My ace had been trumped.

Stunned, I proceeded down the induction line past other test stations. I could hear that old war time song ringing in my head.

You're in the army now!
You're in the army now!
You'll never get rich, you son of a b—h!
You're in the army NOW!

The regimentation learned at Sacred Heart School came in handy during boot camp. I quietly avoided conflict, volunteered for nothing and followed instructions, knowing full well that at the end of boot camp (something everyone had to endure) there was a soft job waiting for me somewhere other than here at Fort Leonard Wood, Missouri. After all, I thought, the few of us in boot camp who have college degrees will surely get placed in our proper MOS (method of service) classification. My MOS was Social Work.

You grow up fast in the army. Boot camp brings you close to live ammunition, possible death and there is the far off chance that some war might break out. For the first time in my life I'm away from home, an independent adult, becoming a man. But I'm here because I have to be. I'll make the best of it and then move on to better things.

Sure enough, after boot camp I am sent to Fort Sam Houston, located in the middle of the beautiful city of San Antonio, Texas, indeed a posh base and envied assignment. Those stationed here can live in the city and report to the base for duty each morning. No barracks, no mess hall, no roll call in the morning. Not really army life. I loved it.

Overjoyed, I forgot: I am in the army where mistakes can be routine. I found myself in nurses' training school, learning to give intramuscular shots. Ugh, this will not work. A letter to congressman Charles Diggs of Michigan is dispatched and in due time I am on my way to Fort Hood, Texas where I will be assigned to a Social Work position.

Fort Hood, Texas is now my permanent home. The area around the Fort is flat like Detroit, but the weather is hot, yet dry and bearable, much unlike the weather in boot camp. Cold, moist and the landscape hilly. I like this new assignment mostly because I am far away from the Macho-ism of boot camp.

"Get in line soldier!"

"Can't you count soldier?"

"Hup, two, three, four"

"Attention! Fallin! Fallout!"

These are only fading, laughable memories.

I settled quickly into my routine at the Mental Hygiene Clinic where I am assigned to do intake interviews. Interviews which precede a soldier seeing the psychiatrist. At the same time I miss home, my friends and Janet. I am miles from nowhere and even farther from real people (people like me). It feels like suspended animation. Little to do, little to see and few people to talk to. Maybe this is what Father Klein had in mind when he described Limbo.

My nine to five job is great though. I learn a lot from the staff psychiatrists. But I miss Janet.

To pass the time, I take a part time job in the hospital library, which gives me access to all the books and material I want to read, AND enough extra money to buy a snazzy green two-tone Studebaker Coupe with overdrive. I look sharp when I "tool down" to Austin, Texas once a month to visit Houston-Tillison College and "hang with" the brothers down there. But nothing takes my mind off JANET.

I wrote Janet lots of letters. In one I asked "Will you marry me, will you be Mrs. Garland Jaggers, Jr.?" The happy response is "Yes."

The girl of my dreams, the woman who was symmetrically perfect, always immaculately dressed, poised, sophisticated with the socially correct manners of a well-trained "Westside Girl." The virtual dream for a tough-edged eastside ghetto boy, who recited

Shakespeare, T. S. Elliot, and Browning, among others, got the best news of his life. "Yes, I'll marry you," Janet said.

Janet and I were married on February 21st, 1958 in Temple, Texas, the county seat, before a Justice of the Peace. It was a short, sweet exchange of vows, so short that I only recall saying, "I DO." And for the next three days I was on cloud nine. Marriage does that, it makes the world seem like heaven, it makes you want to smile and shout, kiss and hug, dance and sing. Then at night you are satisfied to snuggle up, as close as you can get, in the arms of your loved one and drift off aimlessly to your private, safe, peaceful nirvana.

Janet and I were entertained by my buddies from the clinic, at the Caplows' home (just off base) in Killeen, Texas. We enjoyed a quiet fun filled evening, anticipating our civilian lives.

Mrs. Caplow encouraged Janet to move to Texas and join me for my last year in service. I welcomed the idea, but wondered whether the segregated city of Killeen and the poor housing accommodations would suit my new wife. We will decide that issue in private.

My decision was made clear for me on Janet's second day there in Killeen. We had gone off the base to go window shopping along the main drag. I had mixed emotions as I moved along with her graceful stride, listening to her lilting laughter. First there was the pride and pleasure I always felt when we were together. But now I also registered how she would be viewed through the narrow minded, prejudicial vision of these Killeen "crackers." Her prideful stride would be read as arrogance, the confident tilt of her head and shoulders registered as "uppity" defiance. I had heard of the kind of violent cruelty the local residents were capable of: my own demeanor and air had attracted many unfriendly glares. I was also aware that though we had been asked to swear to defend this country, the army had a poor record of defending Black GI's against white populace or even against white GI's. So I was uneasy as we strolled by the narrowing eyes of Killeen's citizens.

"Oh, look Garland." Janet's eye had been caught by a ring in the window of a jewelry shop. "Let's go in and price it!"

We started into the door, the white salesclerk blocked the way. "We aren't open to your kind."

"What do you mean my kind?" Janet was infuriated.

"You know what I mean. No Nigras!"

Janet told me later that the euphemism, nigra, sounded like plain old nigger to her. So, being a Detroit sister, her mother's daughter to the bone, she shifted to attack mode, ready to take a swing, with a right hand Joe Louis punch. I grabbed her, pulled her back against my chest.

"No Janet, no. Come on, baby. Let's go." She strained toward him again. It was all I could to hold her, I whisper in her ear, "They still lynch us down here, Janet. And the army don't give a damn." We slowly backed away as the store-owner came out to the sidewalk to tell others about the two uppity Northern Negroes who had actually wanted to enter his shop.

After Janet had done some venting, we were silent all the way back to the camp. We spent the next day on base in a special silence weighted with pain, embarrassment, and a sense of impotence, familiar to Black Americans and referred to as the "the blues." Which seems to be another euphemism.

The next day I could not get to the airport fast enough to get

Janet on a plane back to Detroit. I knew that if she stayed, with her fighter's heart and temper, she would confront the prejudice again. I would have to protect her. No, we would not live in Killeen. I would join Janet in Detroit, after my discharge

Chapter 8

I awoke at 6:00 am on February 6th, 1959, dressed, went to my car, cranked it up and headed north. All my worldly goods stacked neatly in the trunk. I am going home, after 732 days of living a life I did not ask for, in a state I grew to hate, doing my patriotic duty. (I did not feel patriotic.) I am saying, "Good-bye army, hello life."

I drove straight through the 1,203 miles from Fort Hood, Texas to 1635 West Euclid in Detroit, except for stops in Oklahoma (mom's home state), and Missouri (aunt Ethel's home state) and Indiana (no one's state). I stopped only for gas, oil, snacks, and a no-nod pill, given me by Dr. Estes G. Copen, head of the Mental Hygiene Clinic.

Night fell as I neared St. Louis and rain fell with it. I kept driving, popping pills and snacks. I was just as anxious to leave Texas as I was to get home. I arrived at 1635 Euclid Street (this is the first time being here) knocked on the door of my new home, and when Janet answered, gave her a long, long kiss, a wilted hug, told her I was tired to the bones, dragged my duffle bag into the house and in short order was fast asleep.

I awoke two days later to start my new life, but it took me no time at all to acclimate myself to civilian life, married life, city life and all the non-army things I dearly missed. It was fun learning to be a civilian. And I never again wanted to see anything Army. I never again wore my army clothes, even on Veterans Day.

Chapter 9

After a week of rest, re-acclimation and renewing old friend-ships, I was ready to return to my job with the City of Detroit Welfare Department. One good thing about army service, you gain seniority with your employer. This added seniority opened the door of opportunity to apply for, and gain entrance to, the School of Social Work at Wayne State University. I was accepted without the hassle of my first attempt at admission. I completed the Masters Degree in Social Work in 1962, and armed with these new credentials, returned to the City of Detroit Welfare Depart-ment (Bureau of Social Services unit).

"Miss Hardy", I said meeting her in the hallway near the water cooler, "I'd like to meet with you sometime today when you have time." Miss Laura Hardy was a supervisor in the Children's Service Department. I trusted her judgement and knowledge of the poli-tics of the department. I believed she would give me straight answers to the questions I was about to ask.

"Garland, if you have time now, come on over to my office."

I followed her to her corner office overlooking the traffic court building in downtown Detroit. Laura was the youngest of the five supervisors in the department and a rather carefree soul.

"Have a seat, what's on your mind?"

"Miss Hardy," I began, "My two year commitment to the city is up this year. So I need to know, for professional reasons, how long do you think it will take me to become a supervisor?"

"Well, let me see," thumbing through her mind the names of the other supervisors in the department, "Mrs. Janes, Mrs. Olds and Mrs Sinkford still have a lot of time before retirement. And as for your supervisor, Miss Ruth Mendenhall, only the lord knows how long she plans to stay around. We all thought she would retire long ago. So, on the upside it could be 8 years and then on the downside maybe 10 years. But, you know Garland, you really can't tell about this kind of thing. It could be more, it could be less."

"Thanks, you have been very helpful," I said, and then left after some small talk.

I really didn't need more. I had my answer. It did not take long for me to understand that these five women would have to be carried off these supervisory jobs. I couldn't wait 8 years: I have a family, a new car and a new home. Besides, I'm qualified for supervision, and that is the bottom line.

I accepted a position with Family Services of Metropolitan Detroit on the invitation of Geraldine Ellington. The agency needed a Black male social worker, offered a nice pay increase and had open supervisory positions due to their growth. Just as important, was the social work approach which they initiated. Namely, Activism.

None of that 50 minute, psychotherapeutic Freudian based therapy stuff, Activism got to the presenting problem; what the client saw as the problem, and worked on that concern – not the psychology <u>behind</u> the problem. It was in many ways a very productive approach.

Chapter 10

Unknown to me, during this very same time that I am involved in this new Activism, six thousand mile away in Rome, the seat of the Roman Catholic Church, Pope John XXIII has called together all the Bishops of the Church. He has an Activist agenda of his own. It is called "Vatican II Council." Pope John XXIII wants to empower the laity (little people like me) of the Church, give them a say-so in the affairs of faith. The Bishops agree to changes in the relationship between Father and the Laity and Sisters. Some more radical changes are debated, such changes as, married Priests, and Sisters with authority, but these changes are tabled. Changes in some rites of the Church are approved and the mass and altar will be the most dramatic visible change enacted. Most Catholics, and even non-Catholics, hail the changes as "good for the Church."

Chapter 11

I'd been working about two years with Family Services, making contacts and building what I heard was a good reputation as a "people" oriented Activist social worker, when I got a call for a lunch meeting with Dennis Bjerke (pronounced beer-key). When we met, I determined that he was a young, upwardly mobile, newly-wed federal employee looking for a Black social worker to head up the Out-Patient Social Services department at Herman Kiefer Hospital.

"You've got the right man, Dennis," I said as I shook his hand in agreement to accept the position.

Four years out of graduate school, I was ready for this directorship. The pay and accompanying prestige of the position was commensurate with my time-table for this stage of my life. As Director of Out-Patient Social Services, I was now on a par with many of my former supervisors with the Welfare Department. And it hadn't taken the eight years that Miss Hardy suggested.

During my orientation for the position of Out-Patient Social Services Director, Dennis Bjerke detailed the mission of the project and role of my Department.

"Garland," Dennis began, "the ultimate goal of this project is to close down Herman Kiefer Hospital [the Tuberculosis center for Wayne County, Michigan] as we know it. Now this is not for public consumption," he said lowering his voice, not to be overheard, "but the fact of the matter is that according to the Communicable Disease Center [CDC] of the National Department of Health, we have a new combination of drugs which will treat Tuberculosis without prolonged hospitalization or surgery." He lowered his voice even more, "There are doctors in this hospital who refuse to give up their vested interest in long term hospitalization and thoracic surgery. We must overcome that resistance. Now the goal of your department is to counsel those patients, who abscond from hospital treatment, to accept out-patient treatment with our new medication, so long as they are not a public health threat to themselves, their families or the community."

"Well!" I asked puzzled at the scenario, "How do we get these same doctors in the hospital to treat the patients, on an out-patient basis, once we find them?"

"Garland," Dennis said with a large grin on his face, "we have hired our own doctor for this project. He will treat all the abscondees you recommend."

"Let's do it!" I said with enthusiasm. "Let's do it!"

When I returned to the seclusion of my office, I thought about my conversation with Dennis. Is this some kind of conspiracy against the local hospital administration? How could the head of the hospital not know the aims of the project? There must be more to this situation than I've been told!

This project, on the other hand, fascinates me with its sub-plot. Like a good movie, there are two opposing goals being pursued by competing interests. I like it, but this is not something I was taught to expect in the School of Social Work. This project is about bringing 19th century medicine into the 20th century.

My gut feeling tells me that to be effective in this new position I must learn as much about Tuberculosis as possible to bring myself up to speed with my counterparts in the hospital. Conferences in Lansing, Atlanta, and San Francisco with the top experts in the field of Tuberculosis gets me up to speed with Mrs. M, head of the In-Patient Social Services.

At the same time I am interviewing several abscondees and learning why they left hospital treatment. Soon, I have a profile of the abscondee:

He/she is weary from the long stay in the hospital, has a family who needs and loves them, is usually kept in the dark about their progress toward a cure and a probable discharge date. But the universal fear is THORACIC SURGERY, the ultimate hospital remedy for Tuberculosis. A surgery that leaves them without part of their lungs and generally deformed and permanently disabled.

On an individual level the patients complained about the lack of respect (being called by their first name), the inhumanity of the institution (being cut off from family contact), and the authoritarianism (being prepared for surgery without warning or consultation).

All in all, I was feeling pretty good, career-wise, that warm afternoon on July 22, 1967 when I leaned back in my chair, looked out the window and saw billowing across the Western horizon the black clouds of smoke announcing the start of the Detroit Rebellion of '67! It wasn't just the physical fires burning 12th Street and environs going on out there; there were all kinds of racial, social, psychological fires burning in the community.

The Detroit Rebellion caught me by surprise. Sure Watts had burned and Newark had burned and there were flare-ups of great magnitude in other cities. But being so focused on my job and family, a rebellion in Detroit had not occurred to me. The week of the rebellion, George Gaines and I went over to 12th Street to talk to some folks, to get a first hand view of what was going on. We both knew what had started the rebellion (a police raid of a private party on 12th) but we wanted to know what had led up to the fires.

For us, the police raid was just the straw that broke the camel's back – it was the popping of the safety valve. Black people wanted control. Control of their lives, their community, and their destiny. The police raid only proved how little control they had.

Tales of police brutality abounded, lack of humane services was a repeated complaint. A plethora of issues faced the people in the community, but at bottom it was, again, control.

I could hear the pain in these voices which I once heard in my mother's voice when she talked about "those Southern Senators Eastland and Bilbo" who openly and passionately denied the humanity of Black folk. I could see on their faces the disgust which I saw on my mother's face when I brought home stale meat from the market on Hastings: "Take this meat back to the store and get my money back," she said with a firmness unlike her gentle demeanor.

The tales of mistreatment rang too many bells in my head. The Emmit Till lynching came to mind, the store clerk in Killeen, Texas came to mind. The codicil in the deed to my home "no part of said property shall be used or occupied in whole or part by any person not of pure, unmixed, white caucasion race"... came to mind like a thunderbolt.

The rebellion now made psychological sense to me. This country has an un-improving race problem, and it's time for me to "get with it." My new found commitment to addressing the problems pressing down on my people catapulted me into the public arena. As president of the newly formed Association of Black Social Workers, I addressed the Booker T. Washington Business Association (Black businessmen) and the local branch of the National Association of Social Workers (mostly white professional social workers). My message to both groups was clear, there are a number of pressing problems in my community which must be addressed NOW, and as Black social workers we demand that we head up all the agencies serving the Black community. And, lastly, we want white people to deal with their problem of racism.

Chapter 12

While my new found commitment has taken me out into the community, unknown to me, Bishop John Dearden (soon to be named Cardinal) is also going out into the community. The Roman Catholic Church, like every organization and institution in the city, is affected by the rebellion, and Dearden knows that he, as head of the church in Detroit, must do something.

John Dearden is the tall, soft spoken, silver tongued CEO of the local Catholic Church. He is a Dwight D. Eisenhower look-a-like clothed in priestly attire. He too, commands an army; an army of obedient Priests who move in lockstep to his marching orders. A liberal Priest by reputation, Dearden is one of the architects of Vatican II.

Just after the rebellion, he is chauffeured along Mack Avenue through the rubble and charred debris of the east side of Detroit, his eyes have never seen such chaos, but his ethnic-Irish memory recalls the rubble and charred lives of the "potato famine" and so he is moved.

"Here is a check for $1,000, Deacon Al," Dearden began, "take this and do whatever you feel is necessary, and if more is needed,

I will provide more." These are the words of the Good Samaritan, I say to myself, as Al relates the story to me. I am impressed!

Deacon Al McNeeley is the Director of the Inter-Cultural Formation Center housed at St Bernard's Church. He is the second highest ranked Black cleric (Deacons fall just below an ordained Priest) in the Metropolitan area, and has a long history of service in his community. The check is welcomed, useful and expected.

Chapter 13

Remembering the challenge Dennis laid out for me in that early meeting, I organized the "Herman Kiefer Alumni Association." These alumni were some of the abscondees now being treated as outpatients, and they were pleased with this new treatment milieu. Yet, it was hard for them to forget the "inhumane" treatment they received in the hospital.

I worked with the alumni and encouraged them to speak up for those still in the hospital. They too, are not getting modern treatment. The alumni soon became articulate spokespersons about the mistreatment at Herman Kiefer Hospital. Their letter to the Detroit Common Council earned them an appearance before them, and their testimony about the "inhumane conditions" at the hospital warranted front page coverage by the local press.

Sept. 17 1968 Detroit News — *"SHOCKING HERMAN KIEFER CONDITIONS BARED AT QUIZ"*

Sept. 19 1968 Detroit Free Press — *"KIEFER FAILURES ARE A SHAME FOR OUR CITY"*

The Detroit Common Council held hearings. The hospital administrators reported on the conditions at Kiefer as did Dennis

51

Bjerke's experts from Lansing and Atlanta. The results of the hearings were dramatic, change was inevitable. Within a year Tuberculosis treatment at Herman Kiefer Hospital underwent radical changes, thanks to the courage and patience of Wanda H, Bessie H, and Pat N., officers and leaders of the Herman Kiefer Alumni Association. A Detroit News headline heralded their efforts.

Oct 29 1968 Detroit News — *"PATIENTS UNITE TO IMPROVE KIEFER"*

I left Herman Kiefer Hospital in late 1968 to join Protestant Community Services as Director of West Side Operations. H. Fred Brown, the white Executive Director, was looking for two Black social workers to insulate himself from the criticism that he had no Black administrative staff. This move, to hire Black social workers, was I think, a clear result of the Rebellion. For me, it was a step up on my planned career ladder. Protestant Community Services (PCS) served mostly Black clients, and according to my charge to the National Association of Social Workers, my addition along with Cornelius Harris, was called for.

The challenge at PCS is different from any position I'd held so far. I have a staff of two supervisors and fourteen social work trainees (also known as New Career Trainees). And I am different; fresh from my success at Herman Kiefer, I seek institutional change. I will leave the individual change to my staff. I now want change in agencies, institutions and ultimately society.

With this new focus I take careful note of the operation of the Board of Directors of PCS. It is an integrated board so I am especially aware of how the Black members relate to the director, who is white. The Black board members are not yes-men, yet they do seem mesmerized by H. Fred Brown's rhetoric. To his credit Fred can rap with the best. He uses all the street talk heard in the Black community, and seems attuned to its needs. He has one other asset; he is a minister, turned social worker. I scrutinize the dynamics of the board meetings. I expect one day to be the director of an agency, working under the direction of a board.

Meanwhile, we are bringing about some change on the west side of Detroit. At Grace Episcopal Church, at Euclid and 12th (scene of the '67 Rebellion and one block from my return from the army home) several of our New Career staff establish a cultural arts program for the children in the community. They also get a second <u>Wall of Dignity</u> painted on the church by artist Bennie White.

On the far west side, in a racially mixed enclave of old Detroiters, called Delray, we struggled with a local city bureaucrat named Peter Schick, titular mayor of Delray, who saw to it that Blacks did not get the city services – garbage pickup, street cleaning and traffic signal repairs – which they requested and required. We were only minimally effective against Peter, but he got a good fight from us.

As West Side Director I opened my office at 412 West Grand Blvd., placed four VISTA workers in the parsonage, hired a supervisor for the New Careers program and placed a part-time Master Degreed social worker in Delray. Within the first three months I had a full complement of staff – sixteen in all.

This directorship allowed me the flexibility to further organize the National Association of Black Social Workers and to form my own consulting firm – Creative Strategies Incorporated.

In my second year, H. Fred Brown and I clashed over his failure to live up to an agency commitment to the New Careers program. According to the contract with the city, PCS was to hire, as full-time staff, all the New Career trainees, once they success-fully completed the one year internship program.

Here is how we clashed: "Garland, Cornelius, we have a prob-lem," Fred said as he ushered Cornelius (East Side Director) and me into the conference room at 65 East Columbus and seated us opposite he and George Allen, his assistant.

"George and I called you guys in to see how we can remedy this problem. You see, I thought we would be able to get dona-tions from all the churches to hire the New Career trainees, but the churches are having a hard time and they haven't come through with the money."

"What do you plan to do, Fred?" I asked (noting silently that *we* are asked to solve a problem *they* created).

"Well, that's what this meeting is about, George. And I need your guys' input."

"How much do you need to hire the trainees?" Cornelius asked (again I silently noted that Cornelius too had not taken the *we* bait).

"George, how much had we budgeted for these ten new slots in our request to the churches?" Fred asked getting his assistant into the conversation.

"With all the fringe benefits figured in, our request to the churches was for $58,697," George said matter of factly, peering through his thick horned-rimmed glasses. George, a fidgety chain smoker, seemed not to want to get involved in this discussion. I suspect George knew from the beginning that the commitment to the New Careers program was a shot in the dark.

"So, Fred, how much have the churches come up with so far?"

I asked, trying to get to the bottom line. (So far Fred has offered no solutions and George seems bored).

"Well, the churches are having a hard time right now and I don't think we will get much from them, if anything," Fred answered, again dodging the question.

"Why would you make promises to the New Careers program when you were not sure of the funding?" I asked, but did not get an answer. Instead Fred related how committed the churches have been since the "riot."

I decided to strike before Fred got to the real reason for this meeting. Fred wants us to carry the "news" to the New Career staff. Fred has not spoken of a fund raiser, has not offered one idea and there are but three months left on the New Career training schedule.

"Fred, you tell the New Career trainees there are no funds to hire them, 'cause I won't do it." I said emphatically.

I tuned out the rest of the meeting. Fred insisted on lauding the churches' support of the agency since the "riot" and retracing the points already discussed. I am keenly aware that Fred wants Cornelius and me to carry the message to the New Career trainees. I am also aware that the messenger is often blamed for the message, but I am neither a messenger nor a hatchet man. So, let Fred carry his own bad news.

We reached no solution at this meeting, but I did return to my office and have a long discussion with my New Career supervisor.

She and I concluded that the agency will be devastated and the programs gutted if the ten New Career trainees are not hired.

My letter to the Board of Directors of PCS indicates my concern about the failure to properly fund the New Careers program.

There are 10 Black men and women who have relied on the word of this agency. This agency must live up to its commitment. "Use the salary of my position to hire some of the trainees," I said in my accompanying letter of resignation.

With my letter of resignation I also submitted my name for the position of Director of the agency, promising to find a way to hire all trainees who successfully complete their internship.

The week after my resignation I opened an office at 8651 Fenkell for Creative Strategies, Inc (CSI), secured a new contract with Detroit's MCHRD program (the antipoverty agency) and began to hire new staff. Over the next two years the CSI grew to 12 professional staffers. (I could always attract qualified staff). I offered top salaries and the opportunity to grow professionally.

One Saturday in July of 1969, as I opened the outer door to the office complex, Tony Brown, my long time friend, fellow social worker, and consummate entrepreneur, shouted from his office.

"Garland, is that you? Come in, I want you to meet a dear friend!"

"Hi, Tony, what's up?"

"Garland, this is Jertha. I've known Jertha for many, many years and he is a brother you should know. Jertha, this is Garland!"

"Garland," Jertha spoke, as he gave me a warm traditional African-style hand shake, "Tony has told me about you. He says you guys are soul mates, and you have your own agency, right?" I nodded yes, as he continued, "That's great. When did you start your agency?"

"Well, I first got the idea during the Rebellion of '67, but I didn't get the paperwork approved 'til 68."

"You know, the Rebellion of '67 was right on time. It was due here in Detroit, and my brother, it is not the end of things!"

Tony chimed in, "Jertha, Garland here is also a change agent. He organized the Association of Black Social Workers, but he is so quiet about it that nobody gives him credit for it."

"Well, Tony, that's often the case for the initiator. Take Rosa Parks, for example. She was the quiet lady who really initiated the Civil Rights Movement, but Martin Luther King, Jr. gets all the credit. If you take Rosa Parks out of the equation you have no Martin Luther King, Jr. and no Civil Rights Movement."

Tony and Jertha and I discussed many things that Saturday morning. Jertha was a very knowledgeable and impressive person. His grey hair and full white beard gave him the appearance of a sage. He was instantly likeable and responded warmly to my idealism and activism.

As time passed and I got to know Jertha well, I found him to be a precocious reader, avidly seeking books which dealt with the esoteric, always looking for the relationships between history, the bible, and human consciousness and often discovering many incongruities and secrets.

Many were the evenings that we sat and talked. And Jertha would talk in great detail about his worldly travels. His trip to Tibet, where he sat and visited with the learned eastern historians and philosophers. His walks through the streets of Calcutta where he saw the sordid conditions of the poor contrasted to the richness of the few. His climb to the upper White and Blue Niles where he stood in awe of the Coptic traditions untouched by time and unchanged by "progress." His standing in Saint Peter's Square (really a circle) where he witnessed the bounty pilfered from all over the world amassed there in honor of the conquering prowess of the Roman Empire.

Finally, he told me of his visit to the ancient ruins of the Mayan Empire and its fall. These tales kept me spellbound and fascinated. At the same time I grew respectful of Jertha's wisdom and aware of his unusual world view. Jertha had a knack for relating these experiences in minute detail, referring to certain books which supported his facts, and giving me names, dates, and titles of the people with whom he sat in various countries and discussed issues. It was not uncommon for Jertha to talk about the Gods of each culture, worship services, and the decline of nations and religions.

Jertha spoke with passion and authority, and from a timeless orientation. His views were different, refreshing, humane and sometimes dour, and I grew to respect and appreciate his wisdom and counsel.

Chapter 14

The Association of Black Social Workers was growing, locally and nationally. I served as the first National Coordinator and as the second president of the local chapter. Creative Strategies was also growing. We received contracts from agencies besides MCHRD (Mayor's Committee on Human Resource Development). Things were going well.

I kept my three o'clock appointment with Ms. Georgia Brown, Director of Programs for MCHRD. After passing over the pleasantries of our friendship Georgia said; "Garland, there are people down at the city hall who are asking if you have any white people on your staff." Georgia, is a Chicago 'Sistah' who speaks her mind. She is something of a work-a-holic who stays on top of details, but I've known her to "party-down." Her statement sounds like a question, and so I answer her as if it is.

"I have no white people working on my staff, you know that!"

"Well, some people at city hall believe you might be violating the 'equal rights' laws by not having an integrated staff."

"Georgia," I said angrily, "you know damn well you guys asked me if I could get Black social workers to work in your centers.

You know damn well that you guys asked me specifically to get Black social worker for your centers. As a matter of fact," I said with slow emphasis, "I re-mem-ber you guys saying 'you're tired of the other agencies dumping their white misfits in your centers.' Georgia!, I've done what you guys asked me to do. What-is-the-problem?"

She strolled over to her fifth floor window, hands on hips, and looked puzzlingly toward downtown, discomfited, perhaps by my accurate memory, or caught in a dilemma. I had a successful bid for a contract with MCHRD, by lowering the cost of service. My competition, three white social service agencies, were not happy to find a Black agency with three contracts, serving three centers. City hall had no beef with me; it was my competitors, the white agencies.

She returned from the window.

"Now Garland, don't get your dander up, BUT, couldn't you hire a white secretary or janitor?"

This is the most wrinkled, unreasoned advice I've heard about the *equal rights* law. I cannot imagine that it has come to this. I am being asked to hire a token white, like white agencies hire token Blacks, to satisfy the *equal rights* law. I realize the easy response would be *okay*. But I cannot go down that suicidal road, and become a victim of the "equal rights" law.

"Georgia," I said slowly and clearly, "the 'equal rights' law was passed to ensure that minorities get hired, not white folk, and I am doing exactly what the law requires."

"Well, Garland, I just wanted to let you know what the people downtown are asking me."

I think that she could sense my anger and obstinacy and would not, could not, order me to hire white workers. She had made her point, and I am sure she was not in total agreement with her position. But the politics of the situation for her demanded that she raise the issue. She did just that in her own, not so tactful, but politically correct way.

As for me, I have three months before contract renegotiations. So, by October, I'll have to put together a strategy to deal with the race problem. The WHITE race problem.

o   o   o

Meanwhile, both my daughters, Leslie and Kim, are attending Vernor School. Both are bright and beautiful, their beauty coming from their mother. Our new home in northwest Detroit is small and comfortable but tastefully decorated by Janet, whose eye for color and coordination is a designer's envy. The drive home from my office on Fenkell takes only eight minutes and life is good, despite the "white race problem."

"What did you learn in school today," I asked Kim. This question was my way of emphasizing education and checking on the material being taught.

"The teacher told us about how great Columbus was, and how he discovered America, Daddy," Kim proudly replied.

My mind immediately flashed back to my days in catechism class. A queasy feeling came to my stomach, more indoctrination! This is not going to happen to my children, I said to myself.

"Kim, there were already people here when Columbus came."
I tried to hide my fury, but I think Kim picked up on my mood.
"Okay, Daddy," she said, and skipped away, avoiding my dis-

comfort, to play with her friends.

I could not afford to go against what was being taught in school, that would be confusing and counterproductive. So, I joined the Vernor PTA, helped organize a curriculum committee, solicited a Black assistant principal, and put forth a program we Black parents believed best for our children.

The second year, I was elected president of the PTA and saw to it that our curriculum remained relevant to our children. Leslie and Kim soon learned that Columbus *stumbled* upon this continent while trying to find a route to the far east, that the people here (now called Indians) *welcomed* him, that Blacks were not slaves but *enslaved*, that the burnings in this country were not riots but *rebellions,* and that black was not ugly but *beautiful, intelligent,* and *creative.*

o   o   o

Creative Strategies, Inc lost its contract with MCHRD in October 1969. My staff, all of whom had excellent credentials, found new positions. But the breakup of this team which I'd grown to care about and respect, and for whom I had great plans angered me, and left me rather cynical about the WHITE RACE problem. It was a tiring time, and so I went home to rest for a few months.

In March 1970, I received a call from a Sister Mary Ann Smith about a position in the Catholic Church. I told her I might be interested so she made an appointment to see me the next day, and give me the job specs.

Sister Mary Ann Smith is BLACK, that was my joyous mental reaction when I met her the next day. This is the first Black Nun

I've seen in all my 37 years. She is not the Sister of my youth, dressed in a shoe length black robe with a string of beads around her waist. She is nicely appointed in a light-blue knee length dress, with a small white collar and waist length sleeves, her hair covers her forehead, her nails have a clear polish and her hose are sheer. She is a woman! I can tell! And she is daintily attractive.

What is going on in this church? Have I been away that long? I asked myself silently.

I remained in awe as Sister gave me the job specs, and told me a little about the position. "It's a new office that will assist Black Catholics in becoming full members of the church family," Sister said.

I submitted my resume in a timely fashion, appeared promptly for my interview, and was selected for the position. I was told to report to my new position on July 1, 1970 as Director of the Office for Black Catholic Affairs (aka the Black Secretariat).

Chapter 15

On the first day of my tenure as Executive Director of the Office of Black Catholic Affairs I am greeted by the Director and the Black staff persons of the Human Relations Department, set up to handle black-white issues; David Rambeau, a classmate from my early days at Sacred Heart, Mary Titley, a fellow graduate of the class of 1950, Homer McClarty, and Fannie Worford (new faces to me). And lastly the Priest who heads up the office (yes, the Priest is white). Sister Mary Ann Smith is out in the field. It is a warm greeting.

Here are faces and people I instantly connect with, and they have no problem in telling me "where everything is and who is doing what." I feel very comfortable with this staff of the Human Relations Department but wonder quietly, where is the line between the Human Relations office and my responsibility? As for the other departments in this ten story administrative building, their staff seems peopled by quiet, soft speaking, pious, but rigid lay Catholics. And the atmosphere was something like that first day at Sacred Heart school – very quiet and screamingly stuffy!

The answer to my wonderment "where is the line between the

Human Relations Department" would take several years in coming. Human Relations would be downsized. The Office of Black Catholic Affairs was there to replace them.

When Sister Mary Ann Smith returned from the field she came to my office.

"Hi Garland!" Sister had the melodious voice of a trained singer. She continued, "I'm so glad that you were chosen."

Sister's petite, five foot frame belied the force of her character and her person. She seemed to be a take charge person and commanded attention by her very presence. What was her role, if any, in my selection? And I wondered how had she come to call me in the first place?

"Thank you sister," I replied, and waited for her next move.

Sister brought with her several documents "Synod 69", "Phase I of Black Secretariat," (the original name of the office) and Newspaper articles regarding my office.

Sister proceeded to tell me in great detail (it took her at least three hours) and in precise chronological order how she had assisted Black Catholic laity to put together this office of Black Catholic Affairs. She spoke of the night meetings with Black Catholics, afternoon meetings with the Bishops and Cardinal, compilation of statistics, research in the library – the whole nine yards – as we sometimes say. I listened attentively, not like I was in catechism class, but like I was at Wayne State University. Sister did not object when I stopped her and asked for more details about an issue, but my questions were few and far between. She was that thorough.

The best advice sister gave me related to "Synod 69." "Garland, use Synod 69 as your Bible. These are the words of the Cardinal.

If you have a favor or request or demand that you want to put to the Cardinal use his words in Synod 69 to validate and support your request, demand, or favor. Here is one of the key paragraphs.

"Ethnic groups whose roots are deeply sunk in Catholic history have been well served by ordained ministers who shared and sympathized with their particular origins. The church has not, however, developed the same kind of ministry to the Black community. This is a situation which must be regretted. Because of the dearth of Black Priests and religious, Black laymen have a unique responsibility to bring the presence and witness of the church to the entire Black community. To achieve this purpose they must be representative of that community. They must have an effective voice in the design of the apostolate to the Black community at the archdiocese, regional and parish levels." (page 23 Synod 69)

If this statement and the rest of the documents are to be believed my office is in a powerful position. As a Black layman, in the absence of Black Priests (there is only one in the city at this time), we have the right to design the apostolate to our community. With Sister's help, I "bought in." I accepted the role of change agent in the church. It is the kind of challenge I seek and thrive on.

This Black Nun had really educated me about the power of the Office of Black Catholic Affairs. The Catholic Church will change with my help, I am led to believe. It is a new day in the church. I am ready!

Sister also gave me a bird's-eye view of what led up to these changes in the Church. At the close of the ecumenical council (a meeting of Catholic Bishops) known as Vatican II held in Rome from 1962 to 1965 the Catholic Church proclaimed a new face, a new view of life, a new recognition of the importance of everyday people – the Laity. The new face included a new dress for Priests and Nuns. The new view of life included less damnation and more happiness in Catholic living. And, everyday people were given a more participatory role in the church – Father was no longer lord and master of Catholic life.

The proclamations of Vatican II caused hope to spring up among the Priests, Nuns and Laity. It included such changes as eating meat on Friday, going to church on Saturday in lieu of Sunday, allowing cremation, and permitting Priests and Nuns to wear civilian clothes.

Priests hoped for a softening of the rules on celibacy, marriage and total obedience to their superior. Nuns hoped for a collegial relationship with Priests and a voice in decision making. Everyday people hoped for control over their lives and a relaxation of family planning rules.

There was a ring of freedom to the pronouncements of Vatican II for Priests, Nuns and Laity alike. And for Catholics like myself who had drifted away from the dogmatic, domineering church ruled by the Pastor, there was first curiosity, then anticipation. Proof would come once we took a closer look.

The challenges in Synod 69 and Vatican II reminded me of Dennis Bjerke's quiet description of my task at Herman Kiefer Hospital to help bring about radical change in that institution. Am I to help bring about radical change in the Catholic church? It certainly seemed that way. Vatican II was aimed at changing the way the church treated people. White and Black lay-people are to have a voice in the affairs of the Church and Black people will sit at the same table with all the other Catholics.

Like the situation at Herman Kiefer Hospital there was a small Black Catholic constituency of bright educated men and women ready for independent thought and full membership in the church. These Black Catholics were willing and ready to step up to the plate and testify to the inhumane treatment in the church.

Catholics, like Mr. Joe Dulin, principal at Martin De Porres High, Foster Wilson, Bill Porter, and Lou Smith took extraordinary steps to assert their resolve to be treated fairly in the church. As an officer in the Black Lay Catholic Caucus, Joe Dulin and others commanded the attention, response, and cooperation of the Catholic Church.

"SHUT THE CHURCH. NOT THE SCHOOL," was Joe Dulin's demand, spread across the February 7th headlines of the Sunday News Magazine. "Black *men* first, Catholic second" was another demand shouted across the bow of white Catholic tradition.

Joe Dulin, as principle of Martin De Porres High School, had an unchallenged achievement behind his demands. 80% of the Black graduates of Martin De Porres High School were accepted in college.

"Shut down Martin De Porres High School," as the Roman Church had suggested. Not without a knock-down-drag-out fight, according to Joe Dulin. "I'll chain shut the church first" was Joe Dulin's 'mantra'.

o   o   o

While Dennis Bjerke and I had the weight of the federal government behind our project at Herman Kiefer, it is not yet clear the extent to which the Cardinal is behind the Office for Black Catholic Affairs. So while the ingredients for change are present in this office, the mission statement of the office, the official statement of the Church, and the Black Catholics affected by the inhumane treatment of the Church, have no way of judging the level of commitment of the Cardinal.

Nonetheless, the newness of the situation, the eagerness and support of the board and my own need to forge a new uncharted path in Catholic history fuels my efforts on behalf of Black Catholics.

The directorship of the Office of Black Catholic Affairs, I feel, is another step up in my career. This office is the first of its kind in the United States and suits my aggressive character, and aspirations to innovate change and empower others. Its most acceptable feature is that I report to a Black Catholic board of directors who report only to the Cardinal. There are no intermediaries between this board and the Cardinal. It is one on one with the Cardinal.

My first challenge is to create the kind of ambience and culture in the office which clearly states, "THIS" office is different. It is run by lay people, it is Black and Catholic. The many inquisitive visitors who come to see the office and to see me are greeted by a sign outside the office door which reads "*Wizara Ya Watu Weusi*" (Swahilli for '*wise man of the Black people*'). Sitting in the outer-office is a charming, courteous Black secretary who greets each visitor, and after determining the nature of their visit and checking with me on the intercom, ushers them into my culturally relevant office.

An African sword hangs over the credenza behind my desk.

Ebony icons of Black Saints stand on the credenza flanking a bouquet of live flowers and ivory tusked elephants act as book-ends for the tomes of Black literature on the book shelves.

A picture of each board member is hung proudly on the north and south walls of the room. There is a large conference table inside the office surrounded by six leather green and red chairs. A tall banana plant rises four feet high in one corner just beside a large map of Africa on which the pictures of all the current African rulers is posted. The east wall opposite my desk is all windows looking down from the fifth floor onto Washington Boulevard (the only true North/South street in Detroit) and the bustling traffic in and out of the famed Book-Cadillac hotel.

The office is warm, friendly, focused, and professional. On occasion I wear my African Dashiki to add the final authentic touch to "THIS" office.

Those who enter the office see pride and passion. When they leave they know purpose and plan.

A friend, Tom Pride, with a local advertising firm designs our letterhead. It features a Black Bird of Freedom winging its way skyward. Board members, as tradition has it, are chronicled on the front of the letterhead and on the back are the "honorary board members:" Crispus Attucks, Benjamin Banneker, George Washington Carver, Nat Turner, Mary McCleod Bethune, W. E. B. Dubois, Marcus Garvey, Malcom X, Dr. Martin Luther King Jr., Carter G. Woodson, Dr. Charles Drew, Frederick Douglas, John Brown, Langston Hughes and Harriet Tubman. (Only one person ever noticed there was one white person on this Honorary board – how surprising!)

These honorary board members represent the strong, silent

statement of the intellectual, cultural, and spiritual resolve of our mission. On occasion, I look back to their mighty efforts at liberation and empowerment for my personal inspiration.

Now that my office reflects the culture of our people, and the honorary board our resolve, I take a moment to reflect.

Here I sit, back in the Catholic Church, after these many years. But I'm not a student in catechism class, and I'm not going to confession every Saturday, and I'm not serving mass in the morning. I sit *INSIDE* the loop and have a voice in administration according to Synod 69, Vatican II and the constitution of the Office of Black Catholic Affairs. (I wonder what the church did with the Baltimore Catechism and all those rules empowering Father?)

I'm back again and I feel like I'm on the cutting edge of something very important in history. I have the support of my twelve member board (no whites elected to this board) and Sister Mary Ann Smith. This is a well designed office. It is exciting and challenging and perfectly suited for Garland Jaggers, Mr. Dixon's Junebug.

One member of my board, David Rambeau, is from one of Detroit's most distinguished and influential Black Catholic families. Board member David Rambeau has a keen and enduring interest in media. It is a result of his initiative that the Office of Black Catholic Affairs published a monthly newsletter titled *"FOR MY PEOPLE."* Our friendship and relationship has spanned two decades going back to the days we met and palled around at Sacred Heart School.

We are able to increase the circulation of the monthly newsletter to 25,000 readers. There are many controversial articles in the newsletter and they draw the attention (sometimes the wrath) of its many readers (including the Cardinal). The newsletter calls for the selection of a Black Bishop in Detroit, asks that monastic Black priests be reassigned to the Black community, demands respect from the Jewish community, exposes American banks which make secret loans to South Africa and publish excerpts from *"BLACK PRIEST / WHITE CHURCH,"* the literary works of Father Larry Lucas.

I learn from these publishing efforts, and from David, the proverbial power of the press. Printing the truth as you know and find it gives you that sense of power. But David has something to teach me about the administrative workings of the church and it's power.

"The rule down here in this church is *Obedience*, and that rule applies to Priests," David confided one day. "But the rule for the Black man is *'TOTAL OBEDIENCE'* with a shuffle and a head scratch thrown in for good measure."

"But David," I observed, "I've never seen you shuffle and bow or scratch!"

"Ah-ha, you are right, Garland." David continued in his unaffected measured speech, "I don't shuffle or bow or scratch, but that only means that they will be comin' after me one day!"

(David knows more than he is telling. I guess he's dropping the clue, to prepare me for the eventuality.)

"You know Garland, you seldom see it coming, but when you go against the man's rules, the hatchet man comes after you."

"Who is the hatchet man, David?" I asked, hoping to know this 'Brutus' if he should come after me.

"It all depends, Garland. It all de - pends!"

David's message was clear; beware of dis-obedience, for the

hatchet man cometh, for dis-obedience is like a "mortal" sin down here, you suffer damnation. If you don't repent you get the axe.

At the end of five years, the newsletter would be technique-wise (thanks to fraternity brother Walter T. Wallace) superior to any other newsletter in town. And, some of its innovative formatting is mimicked by a major newspaper. This newsletter functioned as a significant organizing tool for the office and clearly articulated emerging Black Catholic thought. That Black Catholic thought and perspective is crucial to bringing Black Catholics together. (Later in 1977, the Cardinal would insist that we discontinue printing the newsletter. It was quite applauded among Black Catholics, but too controversial among white Catholics.)

Archie Perry, another board member, was instrumental over the years in helping increase Black vocations (recruiting men and women to the priesthood and sisterhood). He helped design vocation retreats and shepherd Black candidates through the seminary (one of whom, Tyrone Robinson, you will meet later as the signer of a crucial letter to Cardinal Dearden). A very *active Catholic*, Archie wrote articles for our monthly newsletter, and became the *voice* of the Black Catholic layman.

Soon to be Wayne County Commissioner, Jackie Currie, another board member, sponsored a Catholic musical group. She also chaired our Annual Black Catholic Dinner. The dinner, a dress-up, place-to-be-seen-affair, attracted renowned national speakers and raised considerable money for the office.

Maxine Knighton, who was seldom seen without her husband Rufus, headed the communication committee which put together the first phase of the Office of Black Catholic Affairs. She and Rufus were the proud parents of their newly ordained Priest/son.

William Porter, a school teacher, and Chairman of the Board, along with Foster Wilson were staunch supporters of the Black Lay Catholic Caucus movement. Bill and Foster had but one message for Black Catholics; "Stand up to your Pastor and tell it like it is!"

Insider, Claudette McMeekin, was one of the most knowledgeable persons on the board. As a parish secretary, she knew "Father" inside out, up and down, left, right and sideways too! Who answers his phone, screens his calls, opens his mail, types his letters and listens to all his "afterthoughts?" When Claudette spoke at a board meeting, I listened closely, for she spoke from that insider point of view. (It will be Claudette's letter to the Cardinal in 1979 that will set in motion the controversy over who will rule over Black Catholics).

Other board members include Allen J. McNeeley (Deacon and Administrator of the Inter-Cultural Formation Center), Homer McClarty, James Anderson, Betty Watsom, Lee Bess, and Alma T. Hall. These men and women are just a few of the Black Catholics who served during my first year as Director.

At the end of the first year, in the huge, second floor conference room of our office building, the board gave its first *REPORT TO THE COMMUNITY*. Black Catholics from across the Metro-Detroit area came on a general invitation to elect or reelect members to the board. The meeting was chaired by Chairman William Porter.

June 4, 1972, 305 Michigan Ave.
(2nd Floor Conference Room)
"Good afternoon, ladies and gentlemen. I'm William Porter, Chairman of the Board. I'd like to welcome all of you to this very

historic meeting. We have a very short agenda today dealing with the election process for the board of this office. And, I know that you are all eager to get to the election procedure. But please bear with us as we give you a report of our stewardship during this first year. As Chairman of the Board I can say proudly, this year has been an outstanding year. You will be as proud as I am when you hear of our accomplishments. And those of you who are elected to serve the coming year must carry on the work. Let us first hear from Mr. Homer McClarty."

"I see a lot of familiar faces here of people who were present for Bishop Perry's visit to Detroit. [Bishop Perry, not related to Archie, is the lone Black Bishop in the U.S.A. and is stationed in New Orleans, LA.] You should know that Bishop Perry's travel expenses were paid for by this office and that his trip was a success. I want to also report to you that Ms. Shirley Hill was appointed to the Board of Directors of the Catholic Youth Organization, so we are getting Black people appointed to boards in the Church, and that is one of the missions of this office. Last but not least, I have been selected to chair the fund raising effort of the National Office of Black Catholics this coming October, so you will be seeing my smiling face out in your parishes around collection time. Thank you very much."

"Can we hear from Mr. Perry?"

"I'm Archie, everyone calls me Archie. You know, I'm excited about what we did this year. I'm excited because we have a national election coming up this year and I'm voting for Shirley Chisholm. You see, Black people have to be able to elect good leaders. This office supported her campaign stop in Detroit, and she is a dynamic speaker. I still have some of her campaign buttons we sold at Calihan Hall at University of Detroit [a Jesuit run institution]. We have done a lot this year and I am looking forward to more good years."

"Now, here is everyone's favorite philosopher, Lou Smith."

"Thanks Bill. Yeah, Archie sold me a Chisholm button before we started this meeting. He's always on the case. Hi! I'm Louis Smith. We have come a long way in the past couple of years. We had to lock the doors of the church before they would listen to us, but here we are. This past year we had requests from various community groups for well over $20,000. Unfortunately, we don't have those kinds of funds, but people in this city now know about Black Catholics, and I am proud. Now, Mr. Jaggers can correct me if I'm wrong, but I think we gave out over $9,000 to groups this past year. So now that we are inside the Church let us keep pushing for relevance in the Church. Thank you!"

"I can see that brother Foster Wilson can't wait to have his say, so lets have him give his report next."

"Well we may have to lock the doors again like we did at De Porres, Lou, 'cause I don't see why that damn school office fired that young Black teacher for no reason. According to what I heard out in the community the teacher was fired without a hearing. She was just told to leave. I am still upset about this 'Sistah'. I want Mr. Jaggers to have the Cardinal come to our next meeting so we can get to the bottom of this. Yes, as the others have said, we have had a good year. But we're not going to stand for a Black teacher being mistreated. Oh! and by the way, I think we should tell the 'Sistah' to sue if she doesn't get due process. Now, we need an answer to this problem PDQ."

"Before we hear from our next board member, let me share

this with you and brother Wilson. We have been in touch with the Cardinal's office and we will pursue this issue of the teacher being fired. I am personally concerned because I teach in the public school system and I know what teachers go through. So, Foster, we will stay on top of it! Now, lets hear from Jackie Currie!"

"Oh! It is so nice to see all the beautiful faces out to this meeting. I'm Jackie Currie, and I'd like to welcome all my Sisters to this meeting. One of our fine board members, Ms. Dorothy Howze who represents the North Central region was honored this year at out first 'To Honor Our Women' program. I think it was brother Rambeau's idea to honor women, and I think it's a fine program. We had a fine turnout and all the women honored were so deserving and beautiful at the program. My fellow members in the Dorcas Society are still talking about the affair and are already planning to honor a woman next year. And last, I'd like to second Archie's emotion, vote for Shirley Chisholm this year."

"I want to thank all the board members," said Porter "for giving the community a report of our stewardship. As you can see from the reports, we have covered a lot of ground this year, but there is more ground to be covered. And that leads us to the election procedures."

Questions followed, the election procedure was explained and coffee and donuts served. So ended our first year, with Chairman William Porter summing up the meeting.

"I have never been in an organization more dedicated to doing for Black people. Let's give a well deserved hand to the board that has served our community." Applause ended the gathering!

On Monday, June 5th, in the quiet of my office, I reflected on the first year. On the one hand I feel very comfortable with the

Board, their dedication, hard work and forthrightness. Yet, on the other hand, where was the Cardinal? He knew of this meeting and was invited. It was important that he be present to hear first hand from the Board and his presence would have shown support for the office.

I dug through some of the Cardinal's speeches, found in the Michigan Catholic newspaper and elsewhere. In a speech in Saginaw, Michigan given in 1968. Here is what the Cardinal had to say about Black issues:

"There is so much in the Black power movement that we must recognize as valid and good. It aims at achieving for the Negro a sense of self-identity and pride of race. And coupled with this is a desire to make use of his strength, both economic and political, to achieve just goals. Surely to those of us who recall the early days of industrial unionism, this is a tactic that is part of the American scene.

"...The key issue (in housing) is the right of access by the Negro to housing opportunities in the total community. Open housing is necessary for his dignity. We must support legislation of this nature...

"The quality of education that has regularly been offered to the Negro in the poorer sections of the cities is definitely inferior... it is my belief that it (the church) must be prepared to do imaginative things to help lift the level of educational programs in the inner-city.

"The church itself in its employment policies must be prepared to give special consideration to those who now are at the bottom of the employment scale.

"...and, the church must play a role in helping to bring about

the understanding between groups in the community, black and white, rich and poor, that can help to resolve these fears."

I found the Cardinal's position to be fuzzy! H. Fred Brown would never use the word "Negro" nor would he rely on "legislation" to address the housing problem. Brown did not mind stepping on white toes, the Cardinal seems to dance around white toes. But, I was most surprised to read the Cardinal's admission that "the quality of education that has regularly been offered to the Negro in the poorer sections of our cities is definitely inferior."

Sacred Heart School was definitely in the poorer section of Detroit and since it was not accredited by Wayne State University. It too, was inferior. The questions I'd asked myself in September, 1950 were now indirectly answered. Father and Sister knew Sacred Heart offered an inferior education, and they knew it was not accredited, and they did not tell us. And now, the Cardinal's statement confirms it all.

I now believe that the Cardinal is not 100% behind this office, but I have the Vatican II pronouncements, Synod '69, the Constitution of the office and a Board of Directors of Black Catholics behind me. As long as my Board is in power, I believe change is possible. Without them, change is unlikely, for there is no one in power to speak for Black Catholics.

However, my habitual efforts at organizing dismissed my doubts. Within the year I organized the Black Catholic Administrators, those Black Catholic individuals holding similar positions as mine in other cities. Washington D.C.; New York City, New York; Cleveland, Ohio; Columbus, Ohio; Saginaw, Michigan; Pittsburgh, Pennsylvania all had an office for Black Catholics. Added to this list were Houston, Texas; Milwaukee, Wisconsin; Cincinnati, Ohio; Los Angeles, California; and Toledo, Ohio. The idea of an office for Black Catholics spread rapidly and successfully across the United States. There was, for me, much comfort in this organization. We shared information, discussed common problems and planned cooperative strategies to support one another.

Chapter 16

The years that follow are just as exciting, challenging, hectic frustrating, and as rewarding as our first year. A few of the high points include:

For the first time in my memory, the militant left and the progressive right of the Black community agreed on an issue; "Detroit needs a Black Mayor." A split in the Black vote might assure that a white candidate would win. So, the groups agreed to support whichever candidate won their collective "Okay." STATE SENATOR Coleman A. Young vs. FORMER JUDGE Edward Bell Esquire, that was the tone of the meeting we hosted in 1972. After hearing from the candidates and weighting the merits of each against the rival white candidate, the group voted to support the next Mayor – Coleman A. Young.

MARCUS GARVEY: FAMOUS BLACK CATHOLIC was the headline of the December 1973 issue of *For My People* (our newsletter). For some of our readers this headline and the story of Marcus Garvey was a shocking lesson in Black History, while for others it was a welcomed insight. Our readership soon came to expect similarly shocking and insightful scoops in *For My People*.

A complete list of BLACK SAINTS was found in a book published in August, 1975 by the Inter-Cultural Formation Center. This book would have made me a happy camper 29 years ago at confirmation time. The book, titled, *Afro-American and Catholic Saints* listed six dozen Black saints whose names ranged from Saint Adrian of Canterbury to Saint Zozimus. There was also chronicled a brief history of the three Black Popes.

ANGELA Y. DAVIS, guest of Office of Black Catholic Affairs, was not a favorite story in the local press, but the 'Sistah' was being jailed for a trumped up charge and needed legal fees to defend herself. We were happy to host a fund raiser for her in May, 1972, but many white Catholics frowned at this effort.

One of the happiest moments in our history came with the announcement of the First Black Bishop being named to the See of Biloxi, Mississippi. Being named to a See meant being in charge, and Bishop Howzes' elevation raised our hopes that progress was being made. I was fortunate to attend his installation ceremony in Jackson, Mississippi, my first time south since leaving the army, and the pageantry of the installation was breathtaking, colorful and historic. When I returned from the affair, few could talk with me without hearing about Bishop Howze. "We have a brother in CHARGE," I happily raved.

When I returned from the installation ceremony, Archie Perry, now Chairman of the Board, let the air out of my balloon. He said, "Garland, the Cardinal has set up a committee to study the office of Black Catholic Affairs. We will be asked to appear before the committee."

"Archie, who's on the committee?" I asked, believing that who was on the committee was more important than what the committee would study.

"I don't know, Garland. I don't know," he responded pensively.

At the same time that Archie brought the news of the Study Committee, I am refused the right to vote at the Vicars Council, a group presided over by the Cardinal.

How can one be struck by lightning twice in the same week? I asked myself. First the Cardinal, without written notice, decides to study the office, and then the Cardinal refuses to allow my vote. All of this is frustrating and contrary to Vatican II, Synod 69, and the Constitution of the office. The refusal of the vote gets me ahead of the story.

Chapter 17

AUGUST, 1970. I arrived early for my first monthly meeting of the Vicars' Council chaired by the Cardinal. (One Priest from each particular cluster of parishes is elected by his peers to discuss church affairs – this Priest is called a Vicar). The conference room was arranged to seat about thirty individuals around tables arranged conference style, with additional bleacher type seats for Department Head spectators. I sat at the conference table. The Vicars began to arrive and take seats at the table, Department Heads sat in the spectator section. Lastly, but on schedule, the boss arrived in the person of Cardinal John F. Dearden. Seated at his right was the Second-in-Command and to his left the Third-in-Command. I was not aware of the formal pecking order within the church, but in time came to understand that the seating arrangement was intentional and symbolic.

Once the meeting was called to order by the Cardinal, two things struck me: I was the only Black and the only lay person at the table. (Isreal Leyton, Director of the Office for Latin American Affairs, sat with some Priests and Department Heads in the spectator seats). I was puzzled and faced a dilemma; what should I do, move to the spectator section or stay?

I decided in a millisecond to stay unless asked to move by the Cardinal. I reasoned that Blacks had been absent from this table for too long, that as representative of 30,000 Black Catholics, I belonged at the table and this would be an excellent test of the Cardinal.

"I would like to welcome Mr. Jaggers to this meeting. He is the head of the Office of Black Catholic Affairs. Welcome, Mr. Jaggers." The Cardinal thus broke the silence ushered-in by his arrival. I nodded in recognition of his introduction and sat firmly, confidently, victoriously at the table. (In retrospect, the Cardinal's welcome must have temporarily soothed the ire of some Vicars who felt intruded on by my presence at the table). I sat at this Vicars table for seven years, joined in discussions when I felt it appropriate, responded to questions when asked and wielded what influence/power I could.

In the seventh year my very presence at the table, again, became an issue. One of the Vicars from the core city put forth a motion to allow me a vote at the table. (I had purposely not voted on issues). The arguments, for and against the motion, went back and forth across the table, with core city Priests arguing for, and the suburban Priests arguing against. The arguments centered around whether or not I should be part of the decision making process, and whether or not I was a part of the Presbyterite (the Elders).

Here I am, the lone black face, sitting around the table with thirty white Priests, dressed in their black suits, while they argue over my having one vote. The fact of the matter is that the core city Priest lost most all of their motions, being out voted 22 to 8 on issues. My vote would never tip the scales in their favor even tho' I found myself in agreement with much of what they proposed. Why would they want to use me to confront the racism of the church? Why had they not warned me of their plan? Can't they count heads? I will never understand why they used this forum to raise the issue of racism.

When the vote was finally taken, my sense of the division of the house was correct – 19 against, and 6 for, and 5 abstentions – I would not be allowed to vote.

I can say here that I did not appreciate, nor welcome, being put on "front street" by the core city Vicars, and their making me the issue without my consent and without preparation. (If there is to be a fight over my right to vote I will bring it up. I will caucus before hand and I will be prepared and count votes ahead of time). I have been insulted by both sides, by the Vicars who voted against and those who voted for. It is not their issue, it is the Cardinal's. Had he not welcomed me to the table? But, to my chagrin and anger, the Cardinal is silent on the issue.

Now, the issue has been raised and settled. I will not attend these meetings unless I get a vote and that seems like never. I have no desire to play the role of unequal among equals. Nor will I sit in the spectator section – the back of the bus.

I did not leave these meetings empty handed. Over the years I learned a great deal about the Church. (Frankly, I learned more about the Church in the Vicars' meetings than those catechism classes. I was able to analyze and decipher the words and actions of Priests, get a first hand view of how things really work). Sometimes while listening to the Vicars bicker over fee splitting (the parish keeps part of the fees for sacraments and the remainder goes to the Cardinal's office), I had the strange feeling that I was back in the confession booth, except I was the Priest hearing the confession of snitching, quibbling children, such was the pettiness and sinfulness of some of their discussions. And there were times when the Vicars spoke on Black issues as if I were not even among them. If you have ever witnessed white folks talk about Black people as if Black people could not hear them, you would know this nauseous, battered feeling that overcame me at times.

But that is not all I experienced or learned. Given what I was told in catechism class about the Priests taking a vow of poverty, I was knocked into an intellectual coma when I learned that at least two Priests in this area were millionaires. I do not to this day understand this duplicity, but I now understand that having wealth is not a sin nor does it prevent one from heaven. After all, this church is very, very, very wealthy.

Finally, there is the contrast between this Vicar/Priest and the Priest in the catechism class. Here in this power loop among his peers the Priest is just another foot soldier, a childish, sometimes self-serving, obedient Priest, kissing up to get a promotion back in the catechism class. He is a dogmatic, all wise, controlling Priest who is master of Catholic dogma. It must be very difficult for this Priest to maintain his psychological health and mental balance, having to play such incongruous roles.

The most revealing information was how the Cardinal charged each parish for loans. As the central banker, the Cardinal approved all loans for major repairs AND then made the loan from central funds at an agreed upon interest rate. The total irony of this scenario is that the Cardinal owned all the parish property in the seven county area, so in effect he was loaning money to parishioners to repair *his* property. What other landlord could have tenants borrow money to repair *his* property? Amazing financial wizardry, if you ask me.

Research led me to Henry of Susa, Cardinal, Archbishop of Ostia, who proposed the concept of "usufruct", meaning simply that pagans had no real title to their property. Are we all pagans? The Cardinal had all the property in his name. No wonder the Cardinal can close a church or sell Church property without the consent of the parishioners.

My curiosity led me to further insights about "usufruct" and this may be of great interest to Black people and indigenous people in general. The United States used this same concept in dealing with Native Americans. Chief Justice John Marshall ruled in several cases regarding Indian Claims (Cherokee Nation v. Georgia, 1831) and (Worcester v. Georgia, 1832) that Cherokees were "independent" but did not own their land but merely enjoyed the "use" of the land. The white man can own land (all of America) but the Indians could not! Financial wizardry sprinkled with racism.

The more I researched the concept of 'usufruct' the uglier it seemed. It is not easy to contemplate the extent to which this concept is used today in the Church and it is even more difficult to fit this concept into Christian doctrine. But that is a subject for further inquiry and analysis.

Chapter 18

The forthcoming report of the Study Committee and the failure of the Cardinal to allow me a vote at the Vicars' table gives me reason to pause. Have I missed something? Have I been moving too fast? What is going down? What should I do?

The pause, a step back into reality, brings me bad news. There has been a slow erosion of my power base. Several Black staff in the Human Relations department have been let go due to "down sizing", Sister Mary Ann Smith has left the sisterhood, Oscar Grey has left the print shop, Dr. Wheeler has returned to the University of Michigan, Homer McClarty has gone to law school and David Rambeau (the first to leave as I recollect) has left. I feel alone and outnumbered, just like that day in Killeen, Texas when that "cracker" insulted Janet and me. This is a funky situation, and I need some advice.

The pause also alerts me to the fact that white Catholics are becoming more vocal in their opposition to the office. "Why do we need an Office for Black Catholics?" some were heard to say. "Aren't we all one church?" "I don't want my money going to any Black Catholic thing" was the bold statement of one parishioner.

The Cardinal, always aware of, and sensitive to, his financial base is hearing a growing cacophony of white Catholics protest. This protest does not bode well for us.

The one person who can help me through this funk is Jertha, my mentor, with that extraordinary perspective and that keen knowledge of history, of world organizations and power. I called Jertha and he agreed to have dinner with me tomorrow at the Renaissance restaurant.

Chapter 19

**Dateline: Detroit, Michigan, U.S.A.,
Saturday July 15, 1978, 6:00 PM**

"Garland, how are you my brother, and how are Janet and the kids?"

"Just fine, Jertha," I said out of habit, but was all knotted up inside. "And how are you?"

"All things are fine, Garland, and all things are right on schedule. I can tell from your call, my brother, that you have something very heavy on your mind. Let's sit over here and break bread while we look at what is on your mind."

He ordered a large bowl of Beef Barley Chowder and a glass of wine. I ordered the house salad, not knowing what my stomach would hold.

"How are the Catholics treating you, my brother?" Jertha asked, as the waiter served the wine. "I've been following your escapades with them and wondering how you have been surviving."

"Well, I still have my head above water but I'm not sure where I stand in this church. I don't believe the Cardinal is behind what we are doing. I have run into some weird situations, and I've lost some support."

"So things are getting rough?"

"Yes! I would say it's getting rough, and that's why I called. I need your perspective. You always seem to have a different point of view and at this time my view does not make sense."

"If I may be direct with you, my brother – what were you expecting when you went back to the Catholics?"

"I thought the Church had changed its dogma. I expected to be part of the new Church. I have worked hard to speak up for the needs of our people, but the Church seldom listens and when she does listen it takes forever to move. It..."

"It has been HELL, my brother, I can see it in your face. It has been hell! Now, let me tell you something which you need to know up front. I think it is time that you understand your blind spot. My bother, since I've known you, your blind spot has been your honesty!"

"What's wrong with honesty?"

"Now you asked what is wrong with honesty and the answer is nothing is wrong, unless your honesty becomes your blind spot. Sometimes, we project our own honesty onto others and therefore overlook the fallacy of their ways. This is something I've seen you do, and it is time to correct it.

"And there is a simple way to overcome this blind spot. You can best tell what a person is all about by what the person does, in connection with what he says. I'm sure you have heard the old adage 'actions speak louder than words.' Well, the truth of the matter is, 'ACTIONS ARE THE WORDS.' What a person does is what a person thinks, and what a person does is what the person says. The simplest way of listening to a person is watching what he does. Now, let me put this question to you; What was the church expecting of you when you went back?"

"Damn, Jertha. How did you get to that?"

"Oh! I have not finished. You have returned to the Catholics and you may have forgotten that you have returned to the 'RO-MAN' Catholic Church. Go to the library, if you must, but understand Roman culture and Roman law, for in them are keys to understanding what the Church expected of you when you went back. Then, my brother, you will have to decide how Roman Catholic you are."

"But, what about Vatican II? I know you know about Vatican II and how Pope John XXIII has given the Church a new vision, and opened the Church to the Laity."

"Vatican II is a most interesting phase in the history of the Roman Church, and I am watching closely to see how this aberration plays out. But be that as it may, Pope John XXIII was a peasant, a man of the soil. More importantly, he was a compromise candidate for the papacy. When the power players could not get their candidate, they elected John XXIII who was 76 years old. He was not expected to change anything, but rather to hang on for a while and then die. After which, the power players would try again to get their candidate elected. John XXIII shocked everyone. He not only lived, but he injected his untraditional peasant view into the Church, setting aside the traditional aristocratic view. This peasant view, mind you, is not Roman view. It is anti-Roman. There are strong forces in the Church which oppose John XXIII's anti-Roman view and are working to overthrow it. As for you, you are in the middle of a fire storm."

"I haven't seen the power struggle you talk of, and I'm not involved in it!"

"Of course you do not see it. You are not one of the power players. You are not a Bishop. You are not in Rome behind closed doors. But, believe me, it is ongoing. When you have time, check out the behind the scene struggle that brought Pope Alexander VI to the throne. Then, you will understand how these power struggles play out. Now, let me get to an earlier point that you raised about 'changes in the Church.' The Roman Church does change. It changes its dogma, but in a way different than you would think. You see, the Church changes its dogma once it discovers that people no longer accept it. A good example is the ban on eating meat on Friday. When the Church learned that most Catholics were eating meat on Friday, it changed its dogma."

"What? What did I hear you say?"

"Your ears were not ready to hear what I just said because your mind was not ready to accept such a foreign 'non-Roman' view. But in truth, the Roman Church does not always sit idly by while the consciousness of mankind changes. The Church is well aware of the continuous ENLIGHTENMENT of mankind. And so it adapts and changes its dogma to fit the new consciousness of man. But that is not the entire story. You need to know, since you are in this Black thing, that Catholic dogma has separated the Black man from his true self. Catholic dogma held that it was a mortal sin for a Black enslaved to attempt to escape enslavement. On the one hand, the Roman Church allowed the Black enslaved to be baptized into the faith, while on the other hand, the Church imposed on this same enslaved the sin of damnation to hell if he attempted to escape enslavement. The Black man was equal in

God's eye (brothers and sisters in Christ), but unequal in the eyes of the Church. If you think long and hard on such dogma, the Black man is one hell-of-a-contradiction in Catholic dogma."

"How can the Church maintain its members with such glowing contradictions in 'dogma'?

"The Roman Church has developed a system of FEAR, OBEDIENCE AND GLOZE to maintain its hold over people. Just remember the word **FOG**.

"Catholics are conditioned to FEAR: fear of damnation, fear of father, fear of sin, fear of hell, fear of death. Those conditioned to fear accept change of dogma without resistance, even if the change does not make sense.

"Catholics are conditioned to Obedience (Obey blindly). Obey Father, obey thousands of Church laws, obey all civil laws. Yet, those conditioned to obey blindly cannot see contradictions, falsehoods or deception.

"And, as for GLOZE, the Church hides its errors, misdeeds and sins with a system of smoke and mirrors. 'These are the mysteries of our faith', surely you have heard Priests say such nonsense. A mystery is something unknown. If it is unknown to him, the Priest should say, 'I don't know.' That's the only truthful answer available.

"But, I stand in awe at how successful FOG has been over the years for the Romans."

"That's too heavy to lay on people. I can't go around trying to convince Black Catholics about FOG. People will think I'm a super-super radical."

"Garland, I am happy that you understand that. I am not revealing this to you for you to preach. I reveal this to you for your growth, development and enlightenment. Your questions tell me that you are ready for this level of understanding. Most people are not ready. Think of all the people you know who are caught up in the mundane problems of life, paying rent, raising families, keeping a job, dealing with a spouse, going to school, caring for a sick relative, and budgeting income, and what have you. They do not ask the questions you ask, and therefore, they are not ready for the answers. Their enlightenment will come. All things are in order and on schedule."

"Okay, I trust your understanding, but what can I do? I have run into some weird Black Catholics at many of our national conferences who I can't hang with."

"You seem unclear to me, and hesitant, about these Black Catholics. Could you describe them to me?"

"Well, they are mostly from New Orleans and the Baltimore-Washington D.C. area. They are very cliques-ish and don't seem to have Black Catholic concerns on their agenda. Some are third and fourth generation Catholics who have Nuns and Priests in their families. Many are light skinned or high yellow and relate more to issues like who will be elected head of the Knights and Ladies of St. Peter Claver or head some other Black Catholic organization. They have a political agenda aimed at status for themselves."

"As intelligent as you are, you are still naive about your Catholic history. These Catholics you refer to are in fact the aristocracy of Black Catholics. Most of them have money, or social standing and/or a long history in the Church. They are from the early freed Blacks who have been 'Romanized'. Because of their color, they are more acceptable to the Roman Church. You my brother, with your Black thing, are a threat to their status. I would suggest that you back off of your relationship with them. They may try to silence you."

"You mean they might 'off me'?"

"There is one universal law of power; 'people with power will do absolutely everything they can to maintain that power, and even people who believe they have power, will do everything to keep from sharing that power' and *everything* is the operative word."

"You are making life hard for me. I don't mean that as it sounds. I just don't see how I can help myself."

"You are in a unique position, much like John XXIII. I suspect the Roman Church did not know what it was getting when it hired you. The Church of Detroit probably thought that a layman could not bring about much change in a Priest dominated society. But, like John XXIII, you have fooled them all. You seem to me to be the reincarnation of Tom Turner. I've watched you. You have made an impact in this city and nationally and you have survived longer than your counterparts around the country."

"Who is this Tom Turner you refer to?"

"Tom Turner is a brother who confronted the Roman church, just like you. He worked in the Baltimore-Washington D.C. area in the early 1900's."

"But Sister told me my office was the first of its kind in church history."

"Sister was right. Tom Turner was the Director of the NAACP office, and from that office he took on the Catholic Church. He fought against the exact same things that you are fighting; racism in the Church, lack of Black Priests, lack of respect for Black

Catholics, segregated churches and white society groups – the same things you have been fighting against today."

"Did he bring about any change?"

"I will not answer that question. I must leave that question and answer to your research and to the depth of your consciousness. But I will point you in the direction my mentor suggested to me. 'Change yourself and you change the world', that is what my mentor said. Now, it is time for me to ask a question. Where do you think the Cardinal is, with regard to supporting your office and its mission?"

"I feel he's behind me, I really do!"

"I'm glad you *feel* that way, but how much do you *think* he's behind you?"

"Well, on a scale of one to one hundred, he is at least 50% behind me and the office."

"Garland, had you ever thought that there might have been some other way the Cardinal could have dealt with Black Catholics besides setting up your office?"

"No, I believe the office was a stroke of genius!"

"When the Roman Church was serious about addressing the concerns of the Polish community, it simply ordained a Polish Bishop, and when it was serious about addressing the concerns of the German community, it simply ordained a German Bishop. The picture is clear; when ethnic groups with problems similar to the complaints in the Black Catholic community became a concern to the Roman Church, it simply ordained a Bishop and handed him the problem. Why did the Cardinal set up your office with little power and little money when he could easily ordain a Black Bishop? Once again, my brother, you were a compromise. The

Cardinal set up your office because he did not want to share his power and money with a Black Bishop. Now, let me get to your earlier answer; neither the Cardinal can be behind you 50%, nor can a woman be 50% pregnant. The Cardinal either wants change or he doesn't. It is no disgrace to be a compromise. It is a disgrace not to know that you are. Trust your instincts, while you are in this Catholic thing."

"Well, at least you have left me some hope. At least we have made an impact. At least it hasn't been a waste of time!"

"You have played a significant role in this community, but I did not come to you to give you HOPE. Hope is ephemeral, hope is soon forgotten, hope is wishful, hope is the quicksand of FOG. Hope deprives one of freedom. Those who walk the streets of life in hope only await the pied piper, or whoever comes along with something that sounds good and feels good. Leave hope for the little ones, the babies, for that is where it belongs. I came here to help you focus on a plan and to shore-up your convictions. Leave here knowing what road you will not travel, and with whom you will not travel. Leave here with a plan. That is why I came to break bread with you, that you will have conviction and a plan."

I was in awe! Jertha had really set me out. He was right; life is not complicated once you are free to plan and are convinced of your rightness. I got up from the table. He had said it all. A burden was lifted from my heart and mind. I was the free spirit of old. Life is good after all.

"Thanks, Jertha," I said, as I hugged him. "How can I ever pay you for your gifts of direction and advice?"

"Garland, my good brother, your debt has already been paid."

We rode down the elevator in virtual silence, and departed the

Renaissance Center in different directions. Jertha went on to his work and study and I to confront the dogma which had placed so much fear and uncertainty in my mind.

Chapter 20

"I think Doris Biscoe is the most beautiful, desirous Black woman in the world. I never miss her newscast," said the diminutive Priest who had come to visit me in my office. Fresh out of the seminary, the Priest wants to volunteer his services to Black Catholics, and work out of my office. This young greenhorn, overfilled with the fervor of "evangelization" (the new lingo of Vatican II), wants to bring salvation to my people (shades of Father Klein, a know-it-all – all answers but no questions). Perhaps to demonstrate his affinity with Blacks, he professed this lust and love for Doris Biscoe (a Black TV announcer). Predictably, he did not ask about the goals or mission of the office, nor did he ask much about me in particular. He had all the answers.

The truth of the matter is that this Priest had nothing to offer Black Catholics. I've seen this kind of Priest come into the Black community to bring "good will" to the people and leave them with "no will" – just dependence on him. Add thirty years to this Priest's life and he's the Cardinal's right hand or left hand man, boasting how he brought a feeling of worthiness to Black Catholics. But, in fact, he will have left a trail of promises made and all unkept. This Priest is a walking disaster for my community; arrogant, foolish, empty. Was he sent to hassle me, bug me, bring confusion into the office? Or does he come of his own ignorance? I should have kicked him out of my office, but my parents taught me good manners. In spite of good manners, I should have kicked him out anyway.

When he left, I went over to the windows overlooking Washington Boulevard, seeking some distraction from this uncouth intrusion into my life. My eyes watering, I could hardly make out the bustling pedestrian traffic below. I felt violated, my personhood abused, my respect for Priests in general shattered.

One half block north of the Book Cadillac Hotel on Washington Blvd. stands the office of the Cardinal, in a stately eight story white granite building. The Priest who just violated me is his representative, and the Cardinal represents the Pope, and the Pope represents God, according to Father Klein. What am I to think about this church? First, I am buoyed by Jertha's wisdom, and now this Priest piles his ignorance on me. I drifted away from the Church because of its dogma (Baltimore Catechism) and returned with the promises of Vatican II. But Vatican II is a façade. It is like a facelift on an old building. It looks new and nice from the outside, but inside is old and unchanged. This young, newly ordained Priest is the old Father Klein warmed over. And the Cardinal, though liberal, still demands total obedience. You can take the Baltimore Catechism out of the Church, but it is still in the minds and actions of the Priests and the Cardinal. I am no longer enamored with the façade of Vatican II, and the internal workings of Vatican II now confront me.

The teachings of the Baltimore Catechism, and my new experiences here in the Church under Vatican II raise questions unanswered by good reasoning and sound judgement. Questions raised early on by Gladys, Delores, Pa Swayne, Mom and Dad echo in the back of my head. Questions which I ignored, passed off or just refused to contemplate. Now after eight years in the Church, the questions I have heard raised for me and the questions raised silently to myself, will not go away unanswered. I am forced to demand of myself answers to these questions. Answers. NOW!

If this Priest represents the Cardinal, and the Cardinal represents the Pope, and the Pope represents God, THEN!

WHO IS THIS GOD?

Who is this God who prefers white Italian Popes, who decrees that I should not read the bible – GOD'S WORDS, who pictures a Black Virgin Mary in white Poland and a White Virgin Mary in the Black ghetto, who allows pedophile Priests to escape justice, who stirs up such fear in me, who demands my total obedience to OTHER men, who waits until 1870 to make Popes infallible?

Who is this God who owns such wealth here on earth but says I must be poor to gain heaven, who endorses my enslavement, who will send me to hell forever for missing Sunday Mass just once, who refuses to ordain Black men as Priests and Black women as Nuns, who holds women in such low regard?

Who is this God who changes church dogma to suit the needs of the Church, who uses the crusades to slaughter thousands of people, who loves Whites over Blacks and Browns and Reds and Yellows, who imprisons and excommunicates Gallileo for teaching that the earth revolved around the sun, who is imprisoned in the Latin Language and Roman Culture, who does not welcome me in some white Catholic churches, who educates whites to dominate and Blacks to submit?

Who is this God who sends this young Priest to violate me?

Who is this God that I cannot speak to except through Father?

Who is this God who chooses power over compassion, who revels in suffering, who does not hear the cries of my oppressed people, who closes his churches in my neighborhood, who let Elijah into heaven when the gates of heaven were closed?

WHO IS *THIS* GOD?

I can no longer avoid the answer to these conscience piercing, gut wrenching, reason defying, life controlling, morally imprisoning questions.

These men, these Priests, who bring me this God have brought me a Trojan horse, a false god, a god fashioned in Rome, a man-made god. I will not fall prey to a Trojan horse, nor will I let false gods rule my life. And I will no longer pay homage to them. Has it not been commanded? "Thou shall not have false/strange Gods before me."

Yet there is still one unanswered question which I must pursue; who is the God of MY father, and MY father's father?

Here I am 20 years senior to this young Priest, married, father of two children, a military veteran, college professor, chairman of the Board of Black United Fund, cofounder of Association of Black Social Workers, cofounder of Black Catholic Administrators, President of the PTA, author of two books, editor of a newsletter, a businessman, a Catholic for 24 years, and this bastard Priest dirties my lifespace.

No more of this.

This encounter, just on the heels of my talk with Jertha brought me to the realization that I must be free of the hypnotic dogmatism of Father, free from his dominant role in my life. I must claim ownership and responsibility for my life, my mind, my soul, my future and my salvation. I must be free to speak directly to God without the intervening piebald piety of Priests.

For one single moment the proletarian idea flashed across my mind, (advice that some well placed Black Catholics might give); "don't bite the hand that feeds you," work for change, work from inside the Church. But the flash of enlightenment gained from my talk with Jertha was much stronger, more lasting and less bourgeoisie. "Bite the hand that feeds you poison and bite it hard." Better outside the whale's mouth than inside.

Strangely enough, there is one thing about these Priests to be pitied; they live in a very protected society, are safe from all the mundane concerns and problems of everyday life – food, shelter, clothing, health concerns and downsizing. As long as they are obedient to their superior they are safe, secure, protected... Not a bad life (if you are the dependent type and fear the vicissitudes of life). But being totally obedient is not a real life either.

So I have a plan; since I cannot change the Church, I will change myself. I will make a conscious effort to overcome, discard, and reject the false indoctrination of the Baltimore Catechism (there is still some of that stuff left in me). I will not rely on what the Cardinal says (he is head of the church), but I will take my cue from his actions. I will stop referring to Priests as Father, it is an affront to my dad and to the sovereignty of my personhood.

I will look inward to the God in me, the God in whose image I was created. The God of my father and my father's father.

Chapter 21

It is through these cautious eyes and now with a sane and sober mind that I read the "Study Committee Report" on the Office of Black Catholic Affairs. The major recommendations are curiously interesting; they bear the undeniable finger print of that obedient Priest who sat so quietly during the hearing. The language of the report is clerical, Roman in origin. It is the obedient Priest following orders.

The first recommendation; "Restructure the office, make it an administrative office of the Church," hits at the basic power of the Board, places the office within the bureaucratic maze of the Church.

The second recommendation; "Mandate an advisory board for the office." Again, hits at the power of the board, reducing it to advisory.

The third recommendation; "Discard the present constitution in toto and write a new one," is an affront to the Black Catholics who put together the first constitution approved by the Cardinal. The writer of this recommendation could more easily have said, "You Black people didn't have enough sense to put together a decent constitution, so let's throw it out and start over again."

The fourth recommendation; "Mandate basic structure of the advisory board," is quibbling redundancy. No matter how one structures an advisory board, it can only advise. Structure can give it no further function or authority.

Oddly, this report is sent to me without a letter of transmittal. WHY? I wonder. My office did not set up this committee, so the report should first go to the Cardinal, then the Cardinal can decide if my office should get the report. I don't know what has been done in this case. This is a trial balloon, I suspect.

The Board of Directors of the office, having reviewed the Study Committee report, wisely decides to write a new constitution and submit it to the Cardinal. It does not cede power to an advisory board, maintains much of the old constitution, and makes a serious effort to expand its membership base to include heads of all Black Catholic organizations.

This new constitution is submitted to the Cardinal in October 1978.

The following letter was sent to the Cardinal on **March 9, 1979.**

Dear Cardinal Dearden,

Near the end of October, 1978 we sent you a proposal that was a result of a series of meetings of the Board of Directors.

Much thought, time, prayer and discussion went into that proposal and in my opinion, I do not think it is fair to any of us that there has been no word from the Cardinal.

I realize you have many duties, and an awful lot of functions to attend, but surely, after four or more months, you have had ample time to evaluate our proposal and arrive at a decision.

May I ask when this interested, concerned group of people may hear from you regarding your decision?

Frustrated and almost out of patience, I remain.

Yours in Christ,

> *Mrs. Claudette McMeekin*

As I said earlier, Mrs McMeekin is an insider who knows the Church. The Cardinal has a reputation of responding to all communications within three days. Her letter reflects the mood of the board, and it gets results.

April 5, 1979

Dear Mrs. McMeekin,

I can appreciate the concern that you feel over the fact that there has been a delay in taking action on the proposed constitution for the Office Of Black Catholic in the Archdiocese.

Many factors have contributed to it. In point of fact, the document did not reach my desk until the very end of the month of November. **The memorandum that accompanied it bears the date November 28.**

Actually I reviewed the document at the time that I received it. While it had many positive and worthwhile features in it. I felt that some further refinements were possible. And to define these, I felt it necessary to discuss the matter at greater length with (my Right Hand Man) RHM.

A meeting with him has been arranged, and we have had that discussion. It has been my suggestion to him, shared also with Mr.

Jaggers, that the committee that drafted the proposed constitution be reconvened and give thought to these further clarifications that should be helpful. It is my belief that it can be done without lengthy effort.

It is my hope that in its final form we may be able to make the new constitution operative by the beginning of our new fiscal year on July 1. I know that you share that hope as well.

With every good wish, I am

Cardinal John F. Dearden

This letter (italics added) gives the Board and me relief. We deduce from it that the Cardinal has accepted our new constitution, but with some minor changes. Since there are "many positive and worthwhile features in it" and the Cardinal feels that "further refinements" can be made "without lenghty effort," we are jubilant, and prideful that we took the time to re-write the constitution without ceding power to an advisory board.

April 21, 1979

Over three dozen Black Catholics attend the meeting scheduled to "further refine" the constitution. When the Cardinal's RIGHT HAND MAN (RHM) distributes the agenda and the constitution, the Board members and I are apprehensive and worried. The document is **not** the one we sent to the Cardinal, but has the notation, **APRIL 2, 1979 (THIRD DRAFT) Proposed by RHM APPROVED BY CARDINAL DEARDEN.**

Frankly, I am dumbfounded! I thought the subplot at Herman Kiefer was weird with the federal project under Dennis undermining the hospital administration, but the shenanigans here in this church are "deep." If there is a mystery of our faith it is this "funk" that we are in now.

The RHM pushed through his draft against the objections of the group. He had stacked the room with a few new faces, one of whom was a respected Black Ph.D. who carried weight with the new faces. In typical Roman fashion, he moved the agenda past one objection after another, doddling idly when the discussion got heated. He then set up a new meeting for the Next Step: put the document before all Black Catholics in the Church.

The situation is clear. Only the RHM could write the draft. He must have intercepted and destroyed our proposed constitution (ergo, the one month lapse between the time we sent it and when the Cardinal got it). In the Cardinals words, "The memorandum [?] that accompanied it bears the date 28 November, 1978." Is the RHM acting alone in this deception, or in collusion with the Cardinal? I will watch. "For time will tell," Jertha would say.

May 16, 1979

I call a May 16th, 1979 meeting of representatives from all the major Black Catholic organizations, as well as our Board members. Thirty-eight individuals attend, and hear a re-cap of the RHM's meeting. The group, frustrated by the tactics of the RHM, votes 32 for and 5 against that: *"The Office of Black Catholic Affairs to continue to function with a policy making board."*

The minutes of this meeting are sent to the Cardinal with a copy to the RHM.

The basic issue is now on the table. There are only two positions: 1) the advisory board recommended by the RHM, and 2) the policy board voted by the people. The Cardinal must side with one position. Will he side with the authoritarian position of Baltimore Catechism or go with the people and Vatican II? There is no middle ground, unless he creates one.

I receive a note from the Cardinal in response to the meeting I called on the 16th of May. Among other things he mandates, harshly; "I would remind you that all of your work is to be done under the supervision of my RHM."

He is exercising the power of his office as seen under the Baltimore Catechism – Vatican II is out the window. Until this mandate from the Cardinal, I have never been under the supervision of his RHM.

Now we know where the Cardinal stands. And now that the Cardinal is out in the open with his authoritarian *mandate*, and flexing his muscle, the game is over. I think!

The Black Priests and Nuns present at the April 21st meeting step forward. They want to lead Black Catholics.

"We feel strongly about the need for direct communication between the Office of Black Catholic Affairs and Your Office without an intermediary. The Body of Black Religious of Detroit should be consulted prior to any decisions affecting the Black Catholic Community, in as much as, we were called from and ordained or professed for the Black Catholic Community of (sic) which it appears now we have been excluded.

"This body is hereby requesting a meeting with your Eminence for the purpose of clarifying views and establishing the groundwork for the implementation of a process by which the concerns of the Black Catholic Community-Religious and lay can be satisfied."

Signed by Rev. Tyrone J. Robinson and 14 Black religious men and women.

Bending to the pressure from the Black religious, the Cardinal gives them the task of writing a constitution. And I must step aside and work under the scrutinizing eye (I submit a daily report of all my activities), and oppressive thumb (I rewrite reports to satisfy the thinking of the RHM) of a tyrannical supervisor. A task I do not relish, but will endure while the Black religious try to get their act together.

On **March 31, 1980, at 3:00 PM,** I kept my appointment with the RHM. He spoke, and I spoke. I sensed an eerie feeling in the room. He looked over my report, doodled on it in silence to pass the time, as if I were not there and then ended the meeting (?) There was no meeting. We discussed nothing!

I returned to my office and called Archie Perry, now Chairman of the Board. "Something is up Archie, something is up! I had the strangest time just now with the RHM. He acted like he was in another world. Something is up!"

At **3:00 PM, on April 1, 1980,** I receive a memo marked confidential. It reads:

To: Mr Jaggers
From: Father (RHM)
Date: April 1, 1980

I would like to summarize in writing the main points of our discussion yesterday, regarding the future of the Office of Black Catholic Affairs. As you know, Cardinal Dearden has rejected the proposed constitution which had been developed for the office, and has requested that Father Tyrone Robinson and others involved in the writing of the constitution meet again with me to discuss the various revisions necessary in the document. In effect, this means that we are going back to square one, the beginning again to try to develop a workable constitution for the Office for Black Catholic Affairs. This will require some time and effort on the part of all involved, in addition to that which has already been expended thus far.

For the past couple of years the Office For Black Catholic Affairs (or, known then as the Black Secretariat) has been operating in a sort of holding pattern, without going through the process of formulating a new budget each year, etc. Because it is now necessary to go back to the drawing board with regard to the development of a constitution and the Office itself, the Cardinal does not wish to continue the Office in this holding pattern for another year. I agree that this would not be a good thing to do.

Once a workable constitution has been prepared and approved by the Cardinal, the Office for Black Catholic Affairs will be restructured accordingly, and at that time, a search will be undertaken to find the best possible person to direct that office. You are certainly free to apply for the position when the time comes, and due consideration will be given to your application. On the other hand, since there is no specific date as to when the constitution will be ready, you may feel it necessary and practical to search out now some other employment, which could exclude you from applying for the directorship of the Office for Black Catholic Affairs later on. This decision, obviously, is one that only you can make.

As I indicated in our meeting, your present salary will be con-

tinued until June 30, 1980.

With regard to Miss Geraldine Wade, your secretary, I will inform Ms Margarita Valdez that these developments have taken place, and ask that Miss Wade be considered for a comparable secretarial position on the Archdiocesan staff.

I believe that this covers the main points of our discussion. I regret that these actions must be taken, but I concur with the Cardinal that they are necessary.

cc: *Cardinal Dearden*

Chapter 22

After my first reading of the memo, I thought it was an April Fool's joke. But the RHM does not have a sense of humor, so I had to take the memo seriously.

The closing of the office is not unexpected. David had warned me "early on" in one of our frequent strategy sessions about the "hatchet man." And now I know who he is; in my case – it's the RHM.

While the closing is predictable, the tone of the letter is not. The letter is, first of all, a falsehood. We did not discuss the closing of the office. But secondly, the tone of the letter is shocking. And why is it confidential? Who has ever read such a convoluted, dis-ingenuous, un-Priestly piece of prose? The letter is the last slap in the face of Black people. The letter should have been addressed to the Board of Directors, not the staff. But then, those in control do not often follow correct protocol. This letter reveals more about the writer than it does about the subject it addresses. It is the essence of OBEDIENCE to the Cardinal, who would never dirty his hand with this kind of letter. He has his RHM do the dirty work, reserving his pristine image.

In retrospect, I am happy that the RHM did not discuss the closing of the office at our get together of March 31, 1980. I am not sure that at that point in my life I could have restrained my eastside ghetto fury. I had not at that time reached the self-understanding needed to walk away and leave him untouched. Then, too, the RHM may have sensed the danger of candidly discussing such an explosive issue with me.

Besides, the letter of April 1, 1980 is really meant for the Cardinal. The RHM wants to demonstrate his total obedience. Note, the letters says, "The Cardinal does not wish to continue the office...for another year"...and "I agree." This is the Cardinal's letter.

I now have 90 days to meet with my board and work with them in responding to this epistle from the Cardinal, then move on.

These 90 days are also a time of nostalgia, reminiscence and anticipation.

I long to hear Dad tell those stories, those old adages he used so effectively to teach and guide us. I long for that loving direction. There is no love in this church – only dogma, mandates, mysteries and threats.

I am homesick for my old cronies on Illinois, and their openness, friendliness, acceptance and lack of deception.

Delores would say, going for the jugular, "Garland, why are you so o o o hardheaded? I told you those people don't want you in their church! Now do you believe me?"

Mr Dixon would plead: "Junebug, you will have to give me back my pennies. Can't you see the 'Whammy' they put on you?"

Mom would ask: "Well Garland Jr., have you finally learned what it's all about?"

"Yes, Mom. I finally figured it out."

By now, I've had a chance to turn to the Bible. (Just as Sister Mary Ann had instructed me to use Synod 69, Vatican II and other documents to respond to the Cardinal.) I now use the Bible as my ace in the hole. But this ace is in support to my needs, it is not used to counter the Cardinal's position.

And God said, "Let us make man in our own image, after our likeness:" So God created man in his own image, in the image of God created he man; male and female created he them. . ."

It is this passage from Genesis Chapter 1, verse 26 – 27 that freed me from the dogmatism, authoritarianism and blind obedience demanded by the Cardinal and Roman Catholic Church.

I had figured it out, Mom! I am created in the image of God. There is some godliness in me. I am not to be mistreated, abused, deceived, disrespected or made into some sheep-like church goer. I will not shuffle and scratch or beg. I am a child of God. My soul is sovereign. I am due respect AND I am free of the fear of damnation.

I recall with fondness the great times I've had with the Board of Directors, and the militancy, passion and leadership which marked their commitment to Black Catholics. Their relationship with the Cardinal has been eroded by his six month delayed response to their letter, his late recognition of the Black Priests, his disrespectful RHM, and his failure to follow decent protocol in communicating with them and the two year delay in agreeing to a new constitution.

I wonder, as I sit in my office remembering my tenure, what my original board members would say about this letter, how would they react to the closing of the office? The more I wondered the clearer I could hear their voices.

Foster Wilson would ask: "Why shut down the damn office just because you need to rewrite the constitution? Did you shut down the Education Office when the Priest there refused to hire a Black assistant when you ordered him? Right! Cardinal Dearden!"

Bill Porter would ask: "Did Pope John XXIII shut down the Church when he wanted to change the constitution (Vatican II) of the Church? The reasoning behind this closing of the office is political and definitely racist."

The philosopher, Lou Smith would say (tongue in cheek): "Who is this RHM, and what kind of early life experiences did he have to qualify him for this hatchet job? The man is perfect for the job; cold, cruel and calculating. But, as to the closing of this office by the Cardinal, he has just put a lie to his own words. Remember what he said in Synod 69? 'Black people must have an effective voice in the design of the apostolate to their community.' Well, the Cardinal now wants to design the apostolate himself. When did he become Black?"

"Does he need a Black scapegoat like Emmit Till [hanged for allegedly looking at a white woman] to cover his sinful secrets?" Rufus would ask.

And Maxine, his wife, would chime in: "He must have been late in toilet training to need so much control over people."

"Who insulted him that he must insult us?" Mr Lee Bell would ask.

I can hear Archie saying: "We put a policy board in charge of the office because the Church has always said, 'we giveth and we can taketh away.' Without a policy board we are dead."

The questions raised by this letter are endless, but the remark that perhaps would go directly to the heart of the RHM's problem would be made by Pauline Adkins; "The only problem with Father is, he NEEDS A WOMAN. He is just a horny old Priest who doesen't know what to do at night except write letters. These Priests need to get a life. They don't know Black people, and that's why we have to have a policy board of Black Catholics."

One spring day the RHM's secretary called: "Mr Jaggers," she said, "the RHM is at Dun Scotus Seminary and wants to speak to you. May I transfer this call to you?"

"Of course," I replied.

"Garland," the RHM said coming on line. "Do you think I can get your monthly report by next Monday?"

"No problem," I replied, wondering why he asked.

"Okay, then. I'll look for it Monday. And thanks!" he said hanging up the phone.

I had long ago accepted the strangeness of this man. I saw him doodle endlessly through many meetings. He often shunned direct eye contact and was a known loner. But this particular day would prove the strangest. After I hung up from his phone call, I strolled to the window over looking Washington Blvd. and was shocked to see him exiting the Book Cadillac Hotel. He was not at Dun Scotus Seminary, that was an alibi for his secretary. The call to me was only cover. It was a non-call. Could there be a woman in his life I wondered?

And now the pivotal question; "Is this the time to turn the other cheek?" Jertha had given me the correct interpretation of the adage. Speaking to a tribe of people oppressed by the government, Matthew gave his advice. It was a temporary strategy geared to help them overcome their oppressor; "Walk an extra mile, do not sue, give him your coat." Just as Branch Rickey advised Jackie Robinson to overcome the "racism" he would find in the National League as the first Black player in the league. Branch Rickey advised; "Cool it, do not loose your temper, walk away from the fight, don't react to the jeers and avoid trouble." Jackie Robinson took the advice, and for the first year he exhibited the courage of a martyr, he turned the other cheek. But that is only half the story.

Later in his career, when the Dodgers won the pennant with Jackie's help, and the Brooklyn Dodger fans were 1000% behind their super-star, and his team-mates accepted him, Jackie became himself; he busted the cheek of an on-rushing white player with a well aimed relay throw to first base. This particular white player had maliciously spiked Jackie in his first year. Jackie turned no more cheeks, he busted one.

I will not turn another cheek to a church which treates me like a sheep, ready to be sheared for its financial gain. The false gods of Fear, Obedience (Blind Obedience) and Gloze are dying. I will dare to stand by my convictions, like Dad, who took me to Briggs Stadium to see the Tigers and Indians play. Dad stood up and cheered for the Indians and Larry Doby. We sat in the stands among all those white Tiger fans and he cheered for the Indians and Larry Doby. Dad, a man among men, had his convictions and stood by them. That is the model of manhood that I will follow as I re-invent myself in the Image of the God who created me and the dad who fathered me.

As for this church which needs to exercise complete power over me and insist that I scratch and shuffle in blind obedience; "I

DON'T NEED THIS, I'M OUT OF HERE!"

I anticipate better things once I leave; life without dogma, faith without damnation and a persona unencumbered by guilt. The guilt which I always felt before communion when we all recited, "Lord, I am not worthy," and when during mass we recited, "through my fault, through my fault, through my most grievous fault" and last but not least the guilt Father laid on us all with the "original sin of Adam and Eve." (Is original sin genetic? Contagious? What? And why am I responsible for Eve's curiosity and disobedience and Adams naivete and gullibility?)

With a new perspective on life, things are going well again. In my own self re-newal I plan to revisit all that my parents taught, all that I have learned in this journey in the Church and turn to my belief that I am created in the image of God. I am not aware at this time, but in a year I will have reached the top of my profession as a social worker and be heading up a National Organization in New York City and making great strides personally, spiritually, and financially.

How will the Black Catholic community respond to the closing of the office? Who will tell them? What facts will the community be given? And finally, when will they be told?

These questions are crucial. My own integrity, and certainly that of the Board, hangs in the balance. Aware of the GLOZE the Church has used, the board and I agree that if we leave this situation up to the Cardinal and the RHM, who knows what spin and gloze they will put on the closing? Who knows if they will even announce the closing?

The decision of the Board is unanimous. We will tell the story. We will write the final chapter. Let the Cardinal react to us instead of our reacting to him. After an all night session, working on the press release, a time is set for the press conference on **June 24, 1980** at 305 Michigan Ave in the office of *WIZARA WEUSI*.

From our perspective, the press conference goes well. We do not know how the major media will treat the story, they are white. But the closing of the office is much akin to the story of David and Goliath. Will the media see it that way? The diminutive David (Black Catholics) against Gigantic Goliath (the Roman Catholic Church).

The major media, *Detroit News* and *Free Press*, side with Goliath and lauds the efforts of the Church in helping lift up poor Blacks. Yet, an eager, nosy white reporter from a small paper digs out the truth and prints it. Goliath is vilified, and David comes out on top, just like in the Bible.

And the truth has set us FREE! Free of our fears.

And so by this year of 1980 over 500,001 Catholics (Priests, Nuns and laypersons) have made their exit (exodus) from the Roman Church, psychologically, emotionally and spiritually spent from its cultural isolation (Rome), inbred white, male-aristocratic leadership and its FOG. I left, and perhaps the others left, to nourish and cultivate the God in whose image I was created, and to live a heavenly life here on earth.

Epilogue

The constitution accepted by the Cardinal per his press release is precisely the same one written by his RHM one year ago. The Black religious have been seduced by, and succumbed to, FOG.

The Cardinal offered HOPE to those Catholics who remained in the church. HOPE (the tip of the iceberg called **fear)** would keep them in a dependent, obedient relationship, and prevent them from an active empowered role in their own salvation. This same HOPE is seen on the faces of those who stand in the Lotto lines, wagering their last dollar on numbers that never seem to fall.

I am indeed thankful for this experience in the Catholic church, for without it I would perhaps not have achieved the level of enlightenment, freedom and maturity awakened in me.

Enlightenment (truth) is an awesome responsibility. Freedom ushers one into a different world (a world of infinite possibilities). And maturity allows one to love profoundly and to separate oneself from fear.

I speak frequently to the God in whose image I am created. And am greatly empowered by this relationship.

In 1982 I moved to the Big Apple, New York City, to head up the National Black United Fund. I did hear on occasion some of the actions taken, and decisions made, in regards to the Black Catholic Community of Detroit.

In January, 1983 Cardinal Dearden appointed an out-of-state Priest as the first Black Bishop in Detroit, passing over two qualified local Priests. This Black Bishop became the focus of authority and the symbol of hope in the black Catholic community, replacing the Office of Black Catholic Affairs (now under new leadership).

Jertha's analysis was correct.– the appointment of a Black Bishop would be seen as *the* panacea for the Black problem.

Cardinal Dearden died in 1988 and was succeeded by a Bishop whose legacy as head of the church of Detroit would be his closing of many churches and schools in the inner city. These closings left Black Catholic families scrambling to find a new church in which to worship and new schools for their children.

Jertha had said confidently, and with foresight, "enlightenment will come!"

I say, in agreement with Jertha, and in conclusion to this treatise, "enlightenment of mankind will come, and is coming, to overturn Roman Catholic dogma (FOG)."

As people become more aware, less fearful, increasingly perceptive, decreasingly passive and knowingly activist, the institutional form and indeed presence of Roman Catholic dogma will be ignored, discarded and wane. Already we have seen many of the 499 rules of Baltimore Catechism discarded by the Roman church. What was a "mortal sin" yesterday is no sin today; vis-a-vis cremation, et al.

The enlightenment of mankind presents a manifest dilemma for the Roman church.

Will it, can it, confront its sins, errors and regretted history? Or will it bury its head in the sands of yesterdays dogma?

Will the Roman church continue to use FOG as its facade of righteousness? Or will it fade into the darkness of history?

Can the Roman church deal with its own fallibility? Or can it not?

Will the Roman church benefit from enlightenment? Or will it not?

I have no answers for these questions. And these are not my questions. They are the questions of history, of my life journey, of reason and ultimately the quintessential questions of enlightenment itself.

Garland L. Jaggers, Jr.
Biography

Professor Garland L. Jaggers (University of Detroit 1973-78) has been an important activist in his chosen field of Social Work. In 1967 he founded the Association of Black Social Workers in Detroit, and a year later participated in organizing the National Association of Black Social Workers, who will celebrate their 32nd anniversary in the year 2000.

Most of his colleagues and peers consider him a snappy, unbending, nerdy, aloof, enigmatic visionary. Yet they know him to have a caring heart which attracts the broken, the humble, and the true.

Garland L. Jaggers gained his national reputation not as a result of his work with the National Association of Black Social Workers but because he directed the first of its kind; the Office of Black Catholic Affairs in America. His office, and the dozens of other offices set up in most major cities throughout the nation, were an effort on the part of the Roman Catholic Church of America to find a relevant link to the Black Community.

Professor Jaggers founded the National Association of Black Catholic Administrators and was both its Chairman and Coordinator. He served on the Board of the National Office of Black Catholic and the National Black Lay Catholic Caucus. His novel, pioneer, and influential role in the Roman Catholic Church of the 20th century caused his fraternity brothers to name him "the *Black Pope.*"

It is this novel and influential role in the Roman Catholic Church that is at the genesis of this biography/ documentary/ exposition.

As a baptized Roman Catholic youth attending a Catholic school, Garland Jaggers was greatly influenced by the rubrics, rituals, and dogma of Roman Catholic teachings.

When, later in life, he was called to direct the Office of Black Catholic Affairs, where he would witness and be part of the administration in the Roman Catholic Church, Garland L. Jaggers found a church different from the one he joined as a youth. It was different because *a.* he had matured, *b.* the church wanted to change its neglectful image in the Black Community, and, *c.* whites did not allow him to sit at the same table with them.

Professionally trained in the School of Social Work to listen, observe, analyze and research, Garland L. Jaggers came away from his administrative experience in the Roman Catholic Church with a clear understanding of its methods of control of its members and conflicting dogma. His perky ears heard the stark contrast in attitudes found in the Church, his observant eyes noted hierarchical church protocol at its best, his keen analysis revealed the sordid wizardry of church finances, and his relentless research captured church fallibility.

Just as interesting, and sometime paralleling his experience in the Roman Catholic Church, is his professional and personal episodes in life. These episodes, as noted in his biography, are at first a commentary on the Black males' experience in America, and secondarily, the failure of American remediation.

One should come away from this experience with the same feeling of triumph and release that Garland L. Jaggers felt when he and 500,000 other Catholic Priests and Nuns walked away from the church in the 1970's – away from the oppressive authoritarianism and fear-laden dogma of Roman Catholicism. It has never been reported that millions of laymen and laywomen also walked away.

FOG — An Analysis of Catholic Dogma is Garland L. Jaggers' journey to freedom and victory as he candidly and openly shares the many intricacies of his experiences with you, the readers.

In his moment of freedom and victory, Garland Jaggers asks the question of the century – the question many Black Catholics are afraid to ask – in response to the one final insult by a Catholic Priest; who is this God of Catholic theology and practice? The answer to this question is Garland Jaggers' victory. For it is this question that goes to the heart of the Roman Catholic Church's historical mistreatment, mis-education and oppression of Blacks and other non-whites, and targets the question of white superiority, and Catholic misrepresentation of biblical fact.

If you are not prepared to face reality, truth, hidden facts and the true mystery of Catholic dogma, you will not want to read this story.

For those who fear not the truth, welcome to the real world, and to the God in whose image you were created.